Juvenile Instructor Office

Eventful Narratives

designed for the instruction and encouragement of young Latter-day

Saints

Juvenile Instructor Office

Eventful Narratives

designed for the instruction and encouragement of young Latter-day Saints

ISBN/EAN: 9783337335960

Printed in Europe, USA, Canada, Australia, Japan

Cover: Foto ©Lupo / pixelio.de

More available books at **www.hansebooks.com**

EVENTFUL NARRATIVES,

THE THIRTEENTH BOOK OF THE

FAITH-PROMOTING SERIES.

Designed for the Instruction and Encouragement of Young Latter-day Saints.

JUVENILE INSTRUCTOR OFFICE,
Salt Lake City, Utah.
1887.

PREFACE.

IT affords us much pleasure to be able to present to the public the Thirteenth Book of the FAITH-PROMOTING SERIES. The favor shown these little publications by both old and young among the Latter-day Saints encourages us in the belief that they are read with interest, and, we trust, with profit. The principal object in issuing them has been and is to increase faith in the hearts of those who peruse them, by showing how miraculously God has overruled everything for the benefit of those who try to serve Him.

If, by our efforts, faith can be implanted or increased in the hearts of any we will certainly feel that our labors have not been in vain.

We trust this little work will find its way into many homes and afford pleasure and instruction to all who read it.

THE PUBLISHERS.

CONTENTS.

LEAVING HOME.

CHAPTER I.

Birth-place—Parentage—William H. Scott—An Interview with a Baptist Minister—A Testimony to the Truth of "Mormonism." Page 9.

CHAPTER II.

The First Latter-day Saint Meeting—William H. Scott has an Interview with my Mother—She Forbids me Having Anything to do with the "Mormons." Page 13.

CHAPTER III.

A Companion—How I Saved my Emigration Money—An Important Letter from America. Page 16.

CHAPTER IV.

Richard and Myself Determine to Emigrate with the Saints—Receive Baptism—The Notification Papers—First Attempt to Leave Home. Page 19.

CHAPTER V.

Arrival at Sunderland—On the Steamer "General Havelock"—In London—On Board the "American Congress"—Unpleasant News—A Meeting of the Saints—An Awful Surprise—"I Want You!"—Taken Prisoners. Page 22.

CHAPTER VI.

The Scene in the Cabin—One of the Saints Defends us and is Threatened—John Nicholson, President of the Company, Comes Forward—The Parting Scene—Good-by to the Saints—Taken to the Thames Police Office—Trying to get the Passage Money—Locked in the Cell. Page 25.

CHAPTER VII.

How the Time was Spent in the Cell—A True Testimony—An Officer from Middlesbrough—Handcuffed—Leave London—Arrival at Middlesbrough—The Police Office.
Page 28.

CHAPTER VIII.

In the Cell—A Visit from Richard's Father and my Mother—The Trial—The Decision of the Court—A Few Words of Explanation. Page 30.

CHAPTER IX.

A Clipping from the "Middlesbrough News"—A Promise Made but Not Fulfilled—The Second Attempt to Leave Home. Page 33.

CHAPTER X.

Planning to Leave Home a Third Time—Leave Middlesbrough—Arrival at Newcastle—Leith, Edinburgh and Glasgow—A Peculiar Situation: No Money, No Friends—Make up my Mind to go to New York—Arrival at Liverpool. Page 37.

CHAPTER XI.

Arrival at Queenstown—In Suspense—"It's only a Runaway Boy they're After"—Arrival at New York—A Proposition Accepted. Page 40.

CHAPTER XII.

Leave New York—Arrival at Wyoming—Incidents on the Plains. Page 42.

CHAPTER XIII.

Arrival in the "City of the Saints"—Keeping "Bach"—My Parents Join the Church—They Emigrate to Utah. Page 44.

CHAPTER XIV.

My Parents in Zion—Arrival of Richard Sedgwick in Salt Lake City—His Story of Leaving Home in 1867—How the President of the Middlesbrough Branch was Emigrated—Re-union of the Middlesbrough Branch. Page 46.

A BOY'S LOVE: A MAN'S DEVOTION.

CHAPTER I.
William Anderson's Heart and Hand—His Early Life, Home and Surroundings.   Page 49.

CHAPTER II.
Boyhood Sports— An Amateur Militia—A Campaign Incident—Will Anderson's Gallantry—Christmas Morning Greeting—The Afternoon Service—A Combat Among the Boys.   Page 55.

CHAPTER III.
The Progress of the Age—Will Anderson's Courtship—The Christmas Sermon.   Page 65.

CIIPTER IV.
William Anderson's Marriage and Journey Westward—He and his Wife hear the Gospel—Visit Nauvoo—Gather with the Saints—The Battle of Nauvoo.   Page 68.

A TRIP TO CARSON VALLEY.

CHAPTER I.
Description of the Route—Object of the Journey—Confronted by Indians—Discovery of Rubies—More Indians Visit Camp—An Inspired Suggestion—The Indians Become Friendly.   Page 77.

CHAPTER II.
Indians' Stratagem to get one of our Horses—Proceed on our Way—How Inspiration is Received—An Illustrative Incident.   Page 82.

CHAPTER III.
Out of Provisions—Live on Horse Flesh—Arrival at Carson—Start back for Home—Description of the Journey—Aided by Red Men—Meet with more Indians—Our manner of Dealing with them.   Page 85.

CHAPTER IV.
Premonitions of Danger—Learn of an Attempt to Kill us—An Indian's Advice—Undecided about what Course to take—Appeal to the Lord—Prayer Answered—Reach Home in Safety.   Page 93.

LEAVING HOME.

By Robert Aveson.

CHAPTER I.

Birth-place—Parentage—William H. Scott—An Interview with a Baptist Minister—A Testimony to the Truth of "Mormonism."

The writer, the second son of Thomas and Ann Aveson, was born in the town of Bradford, Yorkshire, England, on August 22nd, 1847.

My father was an honest, hard-working man; he was not a believer in any particular religion. My mother was more religiously inclined; her maiden name was Fawcett. Both my father and mother were strict in training their family, which consisted of nine children (seven sons and two daughters), five of whom are now dead.

In the early part of 1860 we removed from Bradford to Malton, in Yorkshire, staying there only about six weeks, and then went to reside at Middlesbrough, Yorkshire, a very pretty town at that time. We arrived there February 29th, 1860

On the 11th of February, 1862, I was engaged to work at Mr. Joseph Gould's printing office in Middlesbrough. My wages were three shillings per week. Mr. Gould was a printer himself and did most of the work. He had only one other employe working for him, and that was a boy named Richard Sedgwick, through whom I procured my situation, and whose acquaintance I had made a few months previously.

On the 5th of the following May I was bound apprentice to Mr. Gould. After I signed the indenture, Mr. Brown, one of the witnesses to it, said to me:

"There, my boy, you have tied a knot with your hand which you can't unloose with your tongue."

The indenture stated that my wages should be three shillings and sixpence per week the first year, with a yearly raise of one shilling per week until I had served my time, which was seven years.

About a week after this, a young man, named William Henry Scott, was engaged to work for Mr. Gould, and shortly afterwards was bound apprentice to him for three years. Mr. Scott was from Seaham Harbor, county of Durham, where his parents and their family resided.

The following August, Richard Sedgwick left Mr. Gould's employ and went to work for a Mr. Thomas Carter, picture-frame maker, and was afterwards bound apprentice to him.

William H. Scott was a fine, courteous young man, to whom I became very much attached. He had resided in Middlesbrough only a short time when his brother John wrote to him from Seaham Harbor, stating that his mother and himself had become members of the Church of Jesus Christ of Latter-day Saints, and earnestly desired William to investigate the principles and doctrines of that Church. He told his brother to go to a man named Anderson, who was a Latter-day Saint and a resident of Middlesbrough.

Notwithstanding William had recently become identified with the Methodists, he went, according to request, and had an interview with Brother Anderson regarding this new religion; and becoming convinced of the truth of "Mormonism," was baptized a member of the Church.

Brother W. H. Scott became a useful member of what was then known as the Middlesbrough and Stockton branch. We often conversed together on the first principles of the latter-day gospel.

At this time (the Summer of 1862) I was feeling more religiously inclined than I had ever before. One reason for this, probably, was because a religious revival was in progress. The Wesleyans, Primitive Methodists and other religious sects were very energetic and obtained many converts.

About a year and a half previously my mother had become a member of the Wesleyan Reformers, and I had told her that I did not think it would be long before I should join one of the religious sects.

I was a regular attendant at a Baptist chapel and Sunday school, and firmly believed that the principles and doctrines promulgated by the Baptists were nearer like those the Savior taught than were set forth by any other religious denomination I was acquainted with, and my mind was fully made up to identify myself with that body.

One Summer evening in 1862, I attended a Baptist prayer meeting with the firm intention of becoming converted to their faith and afterwards applying for baptism. I was under the impression that they made converts in the same way the Methodists did, but found I was mistaken.

At the close of the meeting I spoke to one of the members, and asked him why they did not make converts at their prayer meetings. He said that was not their mode of receiving members; he told me that when he joined the Baptists he prayed to his Heavenly Father for the forgiveness of his sins, and after doing so he felt an inward feeling of happiness, which proved to him that his sins were forgiven; he said after informing his minister to that effect he was baptized. The young man asked me to see the minister. I did as he wished me, and the minister appointed the following Saturday evening for an interview with him.

According to promise, I went to his house at the appointed time and was invited into the parlor. The minister's name was William Bontems. He appeared to me to be a very good man. We were alone in the parlor and conversed together for quite a while. He told me I must pray to the Lord and get forgiveness of my sins, and then I could receive baptism. Another appointment was made for me to see him in one week from that day.

I went home, thinking seriously over the matter. That night I retired to rest a little earlier than usual. As soon as I entered my bed-room I prayed most fervently and humbly to my Heavenly Father, asking Him to forgive my sins and to produce that happy feeling within my bosom which others realized before receiving baptism. I spent about fifteen minutes, at least, in prayer but experienced no happy feeling whatever.

Next evening I again engaged in secret prayer, but realized no benefit. I tried this for a week, with no marked effect. At the end of the week I again went to the minister: told him I had prayed every night, but found no relief; and asked him if he could not pray for me. He replied:

"If all the ministers in the world were to pray for you they could not save you."

After further conversation he requested me to continue my prayers, believing the Lord would answer. I did as he told me several nights more, but without success.

As soon as William H. Scott was identified with the Latter-day Saints he became a zealous and energetic member, and was desirous that all those whom he was acquainted with should embrace the gospel. Working together in the same establishment—in the same room—we had a good opportunity to converse upon any topic that presented itself. I told William concerning my interviews with the Baptist minister, and that I had been praying nightly to the Lord to obtain forgiveness of my sins, but, seemingly, without effect.

William listened attentively and eagerly to my story. He had wished, hoped and even prayed that I should be convinced of the latter-day gospel. But I told him I could not see clearly into the principles taught by the Latter-day Saints.

One evening shortly after this (the early part of August, I think) feeling as if my continued prayers for a newness of heart were in vain, I made up my mind to try once more, and if I experienced no difference, would give up the idea of becoming identified with the Baptists and would try the "Mormons."

That same morning while at work, William conversed with me again on the principles advocated by the Latter-day Saints, and smilingly said:

"You'll have to join the 'Mormons.'"

While conversing with him I experienced a heavenly feeling; a mist came over me; I felt within me an influence I had never before realized. The principles and doctrines of the latter-day gospel came clearly before me. The Spirit of the Lord was with me, and I received a testimony of the truth of "Mormonism"—a testimony which I shall never forget. I was supremely happy, rejoicing wi h "joy unspeakable." I told William I was ready for baptism and asked him to introduce me to the Saints the next Sunday.

CHAPTER II.

THE FIRST LATTER-DAY SAINT MEETING—WILLIAM H. SCOTT HAS AN INTERVIEW WITH MY MOTHER—SHE FORBIDS ME HAVING ANYTHING TO DO WITH THE "MORMONS."

It was on the Sunday following when I attended the first Latter-day Saint meeting, having received permission to do so from my parents. That morning I went as usual to the Baptist Sunday school, but did not enjoy myself as much as heretofore. This I attributed to my lack of faith in their doctrines. Knowing "Mormonism" to be true, I could gain no satisfaction from any other source.

The place where the Latter-day Saint meeting was to be held was at a small village called Eston, about four miles from Middlesbrough. Our company left town for that place about 1 o'clock p.m., and consisted of William Littlefair, president of the Middlesbrough and Stockton branch, Thomas Watson, secretary of the branch, William H. Scott and myself. It was one of the happiest afternoons I ever spent. We were soon out of town, tripping along through lovely green fields bedecked with flowers of various kinds. Being very much interested in the conversation of President Littlefair and the other brethren—of course it was mostly pertaining to the gospel—the time passed away quickly and we soon arrived at Eston, where the meeting was to be held at the house of a sister named Fewster.

The meeting was opened with an appropriate hymn, then prayer by one of the brethren. The sacrament was administered, and the hymn commencing,

"O, God, the Eternal Father,
Who dwells amid the sky,"

was sung.

The time was mostly occupied by President Littlefair. As this was the first meeting attended by me and the first time I had heard the gospel preached I listened attentively to the words of the speakers.

After meeting we partook of tea with Sister Fewster, during which we enjoyed a pleasant, sociable chat. Then we returned homeward, arriving in Middlesbrough about 6 o'clock in the evening.

While penning this brief narrative I cannot help reflecting upon the present time. Passing along to my Sunday meetings I often see a number of boys, about my age at that time, and some older ones, loitering about the streets, breaking the Sabbath, neglecting to attend worship, and many who never even visit Sunday school They have not the love for their religion, which filled my heart at their age. These remarks apply not only to the young, but also to others more advanced in years, who often neglect their meetings, excusing themselves on one frivolous pretext or another.

William H. Scott told President Littlefair that I desired baptism. The president said as I was under age that rite could not be administered to me. It was necessary for me to first obtain permission from my parents. Thinking the best way to get their consent would be for William to talk to my mother on the subject of "Mormonism," I arranged an interview with her. Accordingly, William went and conversed with her on the first principles of the gospel. It was on a Thursday night. She was interested and listened attentively to the teachings of the young preacher, for he was but a young man, seventeen years of age. At the close of the interview it was agreed upon that in a week's time he should pay her another visit. The appointment was promptly kept, and at its close William gained my mother's consent to my baptism. The next night, Friday, my father, on being consulted, said he was willing for me to do as I pleased.

As everything seemed to be working in my favor, I sought my mother's consent, before retiring to rest on Saturday night, to attend another meeting of the Saints, which was to be held in the afternoon of the next day. Judge of my surprise on being told by her that she did not wish me to have anything more to do with so deluded a people, giving them a bad name and saying:

"I would rather bury you in the churchyard than have you join the Mormons."

Too full of grief to make any reply to her remarks, with drooping head and aching heart I slowly went up-stairs to my bed chamber and there knelt and prayed humbly and fervently to my Heavenly Father, while the tears rolled down my cheeks.

Restlessly I lay upon my bed. "I would rather bury you in the churchyard than have you join the Mormons." Oh, how these words rang in my ears! I had never been so tried before in my life. The knowledge that "Mormonism" was true was firm in my heart, for I had received a testimony and was very anxious to get baptized; but my hopes now were blighted. What course should I pursue? I was young—just approaching my fifteenth birthday—and still under the control of my parents, whom I desired to obey in all things. But could I give up "Mormonism" and deny the testimony I had received? No, the Lord helping me, I would never do that.

Then, again, my temporal position weighed upon my heart. I had recently been apprenticed in the printing business for seven years; and the laws of the country compelled me to serve out this time.

And thus query after query arose in my mind for some length of time, until at last, tired out, sleep closed my eyelids.

Instead of going to Sunday school on the following morning I went to see W. H. Scott and related to him what had transpired. He sympathized with me in my troubled state. advice to me was:

It afterwards came to my knowledge that my mother had been making inquiries of her minister and members of the Wesleyan Reformers in regard to what kind of people the "Mormons" were and what was their belief; and the false statements she received in reply accounted for the unkind answer she gave me.

I went to the Latter-day Saints' meeting whenever opportunity offered, but was very cautious not to inform my parents.

Sometimes I attended meetings at Eston and Stockton (both places being about four miles from home) as well as at Middlesbrough.

I soon left my former Sunday school and began attending another of the same persuasion, but differing on some points of doctrine. Then I attended the Unitarian school, where their exercises partook of a secular as well as of a religious nature. From there I went to the Wesleyans; but wherever I roamed no true spiritual enjoyment could be found as at the meetings of the Latter-day Saints.

CHAPTER III.

A COMPANION—HOW I SAVED MY EMIGRATION MONEY—
AN IMPORTANT LETTER FROM AMERICA.

MY acquaintance with the Sedgwick family, which had been interrupted as related in a previous chapter, was again renewed in the Summer of 1863. From that time the friendship existing between Richard, and myself was of the most intimate character. It was not long before the subject of "Mormonism" was broached to Richard, and he was soon convinced of the truth of the latter-day gospel. Being also under age he was placed in the same condition as myself—neither of us could avail ourselves of the ordinance of baptism.

Like the rest of the Saints, after embracing the gospel, the spirit of gathering came strongly upon us, and we felt desirous of emigrating at some future day to the land of Zion. In order to do this, it became necessary for Richard and myself to obtain means for that purpose.

About the latter part of 1862, my employer, Mr. Joseph Gould, purchased a weekly newspaper, called the *Middlesbrough News*. It was printed on Thursday nights, and necessitated my working most of that night every week. The money obtained by overwork enabled me to make deposits in the Perpetual Emigration Fund, the first instalment being eleven shillings. This was on December 15, 1863.

The recollection of the first night's work is still fresh in my memory: It was till half-past 5 o'clock in the morning, for which I received one shilling. Just think of it, boys! For ten hours' work I received twenty-four cents—all in cash! Would you not think "hard times" had come again if you had to labor so long for such a small amount, especially if you were endeavoring to save means to emigrate? From this time my employer agreed to pay me three halfpence an hour—three cents. Shortly after it was raised to twopence (four cents); then to threepence (six cents). The latter was the highest amount received by me for overwork.

Besides the money earned by overwork, I had a little pocket money given me out of my weekly wages. My mother was not aware that I devoted these means for emigration purposes, but had an idea I had some money saved up. It was the usual custom to go to town on Saturday evenings, and she believed a portion of my gains was spent there. In this she judged wrongly.

My companion, Richard, was working for Mr. Carter, the picture-frame maker. He, like myself, was saving money for the same purpose. He put away most of what he received from his parents as pocket money, and sometimes earned a little by overwork.

From the time my mother forbade my associating with the "Mormons" till the Spring of 1866 (three years) was an unpleasant period of my life. It is true the meetings of the Saints were times of refreshing to me, for I loved my religion; but the fear that my parents would discover my attachment to the Latter-day Saints was ever a source of dread. My home was no longer a home to me. Disobedience to my mother's wishes was ever a sore affliction.

Whenever there was an opportunity for my companion and myself to attend a Latter-day Saint meeting, we did so; but when we had not that privilege, if the weather was fine, we visited the cemetery, the docks, or other places of interest in Middlesbrough and vicinity. These were days which will not easily be forgotten.

In the early part of February, 1866, my mother received a letter from America, which stated that some of her relatives were desirous our family should come to reside with them, and intimated they would send our passage money to cross the ocean.

This was good news to my mother, as she was very anxious, and had been for some time, to go to that land. She was the only one of her father's family remaining in England, the rest having previously emigrated.

There was one thing which prevented our family from emigrating: I had three more years of my apprenticeship to serve. In an interview between Mr. Gould and my mother respecting canceling my indentures, he declined doing so. Under these circumstances it was thought best for the family to remain for a season.

Poor woman! She little contemplated that for the last three years and a half I had been carefully saving means to emigrate to Utah, and intended to leave the coming Spring!

CHAPTER IV.

Richard and Myself Determine to Emigrate with the Saints—Receive Baptism—The Notification Papers—First Attempt to Leave Home.

In the Spring of 1866, Richard Sedgwick and myself fully resolved to leave our homes and emigrate to Utah. I had managed to get means enough to take me to the frontier, where the mule and ox teams started to cross the plains to Salt Lake. Richard had only sufficient to take him to New York, where he expected to stay awhile and then proceed to Utah. The time for our departure was drawing near, and we very anxiously looked forward to it with great interest.

As it was my intention to soon leave for Utah, it was deeemed advisible by President Littlefair that I should get baptized. Accordingly, on the morning of March 24, 1866, in the River Tees, that ordinance was attended to by Elder John Scott; and I was confirmed by President Littlefair in the afternoon.

My parents knew nothing about it. Nearly every Sunday morning I was in the habit of going early for milk to a small village called Newport. That morning I proceeded as usual, taking with me a small tin bucket. I went to the residence of the Scott family and called for William and others of the family. Richard also accompanied us. On starting out, it commenced to rain, but by the time we arrived at the river side it cleared up. About half a dozen were present. After singing a hymn, prayer was offered and baptism was performed. Another hymn was sung and we started homeward, chatting pleasantly together.

Richard was baptized a few days later. Arrangements were made that William, Richard and myself should sail on the third ship that season, the *American Congress*, and accordingly we sent our deposit money to secure a berth on that vessel. Every day we were expecting our notification papers, which would inform us what day the ship would start. They came on the 13th of May of that year.

We held meeting that day at Sister Jane Scott's, at whose house the meetings were held from the time the Scott family arrived in Middlesbrough, in 1863. Just prior to the arrival of Thomas Watson, clerk of the branch, I was remarking on the heat of the room. On his entry, William H. Scott asked him:

"Have you brought the *Millennial Stars?*"

"Yes," said Brother Watson, "and the notification papers, too."

As soon as he uttered these words a nervous feeling crept over me; I felt cold and went to the fire-place to warm me.

We held our usual testimony meeting, and among those who bore testimony to the truth of the latter-day work I was one, and while doing so the tears trickled down my cheeks.

The notification papers stated that the *American Congress* would sail from London on the 23rd of May, which gave us ten days' notice.

A day or two after this William H. Scott received a letter, stating that a small company of Saints would leave Sunderland by steamer on the next Saturday morning, May 19th, for London, from which place the *American Congress* had to leave on the 23rd of that month. We thought this would be a good opportunity to go on this route, as it was much cheaper by this means than by rail. To do this we would have to leave Middlesbrough on the evening of May 18th, five days before the ship would sail.

We were in a rather peculiar situation, and wondered what excuse we could give our parents and employers to be absent a few days without them suspecting our intentions.

To make matters worse, our right-hand man, William H. Scott, received a letter from President Brigham Young, Jr., at Liverpool, assigning him a mission. This was unpleasant news to both Richard and myself, for to start on our journey without him was almost like being left without a shepherd.

As it could not be avoided, however, we determined to make the best of it and leave on Friday evening, the 18th.

On Wednesday evening, the 16th, I broached the subject of being away two days. I told my parents I wished to go with Richard Sedgwick to Hartlepool the following Friday, on a visit to some of his friends, and return on the following Sunday evening. My father was a little opposed to my going, but my mother was favorably inclined. Hartlepool was about twelve miles from Middlesbrough, and Sunderland was over forty.

Having secured the consent of my parents to be away from home two days, the next thing was to see my employer. It so happened that we were very busy at the printing business, and to ask for a holiday would be almost absurd. We were bent on leaving on the Friday night, and go we must. But what bothered me most was what excuse I could give my employer to be away. To tell him the same story as I had told my parents would hardly do, as he might say I could go there some other time when we were not quite so busy. Finally, on Thursday, the 17th, I saw Mr. Gould and told him I wished to go and see some of my relatives at Bradford, who were going to remove from that place and desired to see me before they left. I asked leave of absence from 4 o'clock Friday evening till Monday morning. Mr. Gould granted my request.

It was much easier for Richard to get permission to be away a few days than it was for me. He told his parents and his employer that he wanted to go to Hartlepool, and his wish was granted without any particular questions being asked.

After Mr. Gould granted my request he paid me my full week's wages and gave me a shilling for pocket money. He was in the habit of giving me sixpence a week as pocket money, but this time he was kind enough to give me double the amount. I thanked him for his kindness. Mr. Gould had been kind to me ever since I entered his employ, and now that I was about to leave him, expecting never more to see him again, reflections of an unpleasant nature crossed my mind.

On reaching home I quickly put on my Sunday clothes and was soon ready to start, but became so confused as to forget to bid the folks good-by. Just as I was near the door, my mother said:

"What! are you going off without bidding us good-by?"

I turned quickly around and said:

"Good-by! Good-by!"

They watched me as I left the door. I hurried on my journey and was soon out of sight.

CHAPTER V.

Arrival at Sunderland—On the Steamer "General Havelock"—In London—On Board the "American Congress"—Unpleasant News—A Meeting of the Saints—An Awful Surprise—"I Want You!"— Taken Prisoners.

I went down to a steamboat landing, crossed the River Tees in a small steamer and waited there nearly half an hour, when Richard came. He brought with him our box, which contained a bed-quilt, some books and other articles.

On this side of the river was the Port Clarence railway station, where, after securing our tickets, we took the train for Sunderland.

We arrived at the latter place about 7:30 p.m. After some little trouble we found President George J. Linford, who was staying at a Brother Inglefield's. We procured lodgings for the night, for which we paid fourpence (eight cents) each.

Early next morning we went on board the steamer *General Havelock*. Quite a number of Saints (between fifty and sixty) embarked on the steamer; they hailed from Newcastle, Sunderland and other places.

About 8 o'clock the steamer started. It was pleasant sailing. This was the first time we had been on sea. Richard and I enjoyed ourselves and felt very happy. We were pleased to be away from home and soon made intimate acquaintance with the Saints, finding among them many good-hearted people. We had some interesting conversation which helped to pass away the time.

The following day we arrived in the great metropolis—London—about half-past 2 o'clock in the afternoon.

During the forenoon of the next day President Linford informed us we could go on board the *American Congress*, but said he did not know whether we could sail on that vessel or not. He told us that shortly after we left Sunderland on the Saturday morning, a telegram came there from Brigham Young, Jr., asking him not to let the Saints start, but for them to wait till the next ship was ready.

In the evening of that day, President Linford went to Liverpool to see Brother Young and make final arrangements about sailing.

This was rather unpleasant news to Richard and myself, for if we could not go with that ship, it would be expensive to wait two or three weeks till the next vessel started; in fact, we did not have means to do so. Not only this, but we were in suspense about being away, for we were afraid we might be captured and taken back to our homes.

In the forenoon of that day we went down to St. Catherine's Docks and got on board the *American Congress*.

The next morning Bro. Barker Childs, one of the Saints who sailed with us from Sunderland, asked me a rather curious question. Said he:

"What would you think if you were taken off the ship?"

I replied: "I don't know."

Shortly after this, President Linford came.

"Good morning," said Barker.

"Good morning," responded Linford.

"Well," said Barker, "what's the news? Have we to stay here or not?"

"You can go with this vessel," replied President Linford.

This was good news to all of us who had sailed from Sunderland, and we felt to rejoice when he told us.

Late in the afternoon of Wednesday the ship was towed down the river to Shadwell Basin, and word was passed around that she would sail ear'y next morning.

About 7 o'clock in the evening a meeting of the Saints was held on the deck. There were some good, soul-stirring hymns sung, and addresses were delivered by Elders John Nicholson and N. H. Felt.

While the services were in progress quite a crowd of spectators were viewing us from the shore, and among them was a short, stout man, who gazed intently at Richard and I.

After the meeting was over we both went below to our bunk, where we anxiously awaited the morrow to come, when we would be out on the ocean beyond all danger of pursuit. The ship was well filled with passengers—every berth being taken.

Early next morning we were up in good time. I walked about the cabin and on the deck with a feeling of gloom over me. 1 told Richard of my foreboding of something unpleasant, but what it was I could not tell. The sailors were busy preparing for the long voyage, and we expected soon to start.

About half past 7 o'clock I went off the ship to get a supply of water. Returning, I came near to where Richard was on deck, and said:

"Here's the water; now let's go and get breakfast."

No sooner had I said these words than a noise occurred in the gangway, and the next moment a voice cried out:

"That's one of them!"

I had hardly time to turn around when a rough hand seized me by the collar. The next words I heard were:

"I want you!"

The person who spoke first was Mr. Thomas Carter, Richard's employer; the other speaker was a London detective, the man who watched us so closely the night previous at the meeting.

Mr. Carter then, in a quick tone, enquired:

"Where's Richard?"

"He is there," I replied, pointing towards him as he stood close by, an eye-witness to what was going on.

The detective then seized him and pulled him towards me, taking from his breast coat pocket two summonses.

"Robert Aveson," said he to me, "Is that your name?"

"Yes," was my answer.

"And Richard Sedgwick?"

Richard responded to his name.

"You have absconded from your apprenticeship," continued the detective. "You thought no one could catch you, did you?"

I replied, "No."

Mr. Carter then asked Richard if he had any luggage, who replied in the negative.

I quickly said, "I have."

Then we all went down into the cabin together.

CHAPTER VI.

The Scene in the Cabin—One of the Saints Defends us and is Threatened—John Nicholson, President of the Company, Comes Forward—The Parting Scene—Good by to the Saints—Taken to the Thames Police Office—Trying to Get the Passage Money—Locked in the Cell.

On making our appearance in the cabin, the Saints rushed up to see what was the matter, and in a few seconds a large crowd gathered around. I jumped up in our bunk, commenced to get our things together and put in our box what articles I could.

One of the Saints, named Isaac Sutliffe, said to the detective:

"What are you going to do with these boys?"

The response came from the officer in a sharp tone:

"We're going to take them away with us."

"No you ain't," said Sutliffe in an emphatic manner

1*

After further argument the detective said to Sutliffe:
"If you don't hush up we'll take you, too."
At this juncture, John Nicholson, president of the company, came forward and asked what was the matter.

The detective answered:

"We are going to take these boys away because they have absconded from their apprenticeship."

The officer then produced the papers and showed them to Brother Nicholson, who, after reading them, said:

"That's all right. I did not know anything about the boys."

The officer then asked for our passage money. Brother Nicholson replied:

"I cannot give you it; but the boys can get it by going to President Young's office at Islington."

Our ship tickets were then endorsed by Brother Nicholson, to the effect that the passage money had to be given to no one but the boys (Richard and myself).

Having our luggage ready for starting we disposed of our ship outfit to two of the Saints, the cost of which was about five shillings. We began to shake hands with the Saints, many of whom, with tears in their eyes, bade us a sad "good-by." While thus engaged the detective seized me by the collar and pulling me towards the steps, said:

"Come along, we can't wait for you!"

With aching hearts away we went with our box, accompanied by Carter and the detective. Our destination was the Thames Police Office, which was about a mile distant. On arriving there, Carter and the detective left as soon as they had ordered breakfast for us.

There were two men in charge of the office, who took quite an interest in us and treated us very kindly.

Considering all things, the morning passed away very well. Something seemed to be whispering within me, "It's all for the best." I told Richard so, and he said he felt the same.

We were made to feel worse by hearing a number of church bells ringing merrily, and upon enquiring the cause were informed it was the anniversary of the queen's birthday. The morning seemed a long one, and when dinner time came we were provided with a good meal of roast beef, potatoes, etc.

In the early afternoon we were taken in a hack to the office of President B. Young, Jr., at Islington, by Mr. Carter and the detective, whose object in taking us there was to endeavor to get our passage money and use it in paying the expenses of taking us back to our homes.

As we approached the office the detective asked for our ship tickets. I told him I would not give them up. There were three tickets—two to take us across the ocean, the other to take me to Wyoming, Nebraska.

Again the officer asked me for the tickets, which I still refused to give up. He said he would soon return them to me. On that condition I handed them to him with many misgivings. It was a severe trial to be taken back home; but to lose our hard-earned savings as well we felt keenly.

Arriving at our destination, inquiry was made for Brother Young, but we were informed that he was not there. We were invited in and told to wait a few minutes, when some gentlemen would see us; and soon Elders N. H. Felt, George Linford and other brethren made their appearance.

The officer then told them he wished to get the money for the ship tickets, whereupon the brethren returned to another room to hold council. In a few minutes they came and said that Brigham Young had gone to Liverpool, but if the boys (Richard and myself) would send their tickets to George J. Linford at Sunderland the money would be refunded. We were then taken back to the police office.

While on the way back, Carter got out of the hack. After he had gone the detective drew close to us and said he did not want us to think any the less of him for the part he had taken, as he had only done his duty. I told him it was all right, we knew it.

We arrived at the police office between 4 and 5 o'clock and shortly afterwards had our supper, after which I wrote a letter to George J. Linford and inclosed the three tickets. Just as it was finished, one of the men in charge of the jail said:

"Come, mates, we must do our duty; you'll have to go into the cell."

"All right," said I, and then asked him to post our letter, and he said he would.

We were then escorted into a cell. Some bed clothes were given us and we were told that anyone else would not have been allowed this privilege. They said if we wanted anything we were to shout for it. So they locked us up and went away.

CHAPTER VII.

How the Time was Spent in the Cell—A True Testimony—An Officer From Middlesbrough—Handcuffed—Leave London—Arrival at Middlesbrough—The Police Office.

It was a small cell built of rock, with stationary seats around it. In the middle of the door was a square hole, with an extended ledge, where eatables, etc., could be passed through.

All was quiet, no noise, not even the ticking of a clock, could be heard. There was no light save the glimmer of the gas from the passage way outside the cell.

We were alone and felt sad and rather low-spirited. We conversed but little. I walked up and down the cell; Richard laid down and tried to sleep. This was a hard thing for him to do, as his thoughts troubled him. Oh, how I lifted my heart heavenward and prayed most fervently to my Heavenly Father to comfort us in our hour of trial! Presently I heard footsteps, and a voice at the door asked:

"Do you want anything, mates?"

I answered, "No."

Poor fellow! It was one of the keepers. They evidently felt for us, for they came two or three times and asked the same question. Then I laid down and tried to sleep, but could not.

We had been in the cell perhaps two hours, when a heavenly influence rested upon us. I said to Richard:

"How do you feel?"

He replied, "I feel happy."

I told him I never felt so happy in all my life as at that moment, and remarked I did not care how long we remained in the cell if we could feel like that all the time.

It was the holy influence of the Spirit of the Lord that rested upon us. To us it was a testimony that the gospel we had embraced was true. Our minds became calm and we were strengthened in that hour of trial. At last sleep closed our eyes. Thus ended a very eventful day of our lives.

About half-past 5 next morning our breakfast was handed to us through the small, square hole in the door—bread and butter and coffee. We tasted the coffee, but did not like it; so I asked the keeper to give us some water, which he did.

About 6 o'clock, the cell door was opened and there stood before us an officer from Middlesbrough, a gentleman whom we had seen before. He produced a pair of handcuffs and put them on our wrists. This indignity we felt most keenly. My wrists were so thin the handcuffs were almost too large and they near'y slipped over my hand. He told us to follow him, which we did, and as we passed through the police office, we bade the keepers good-by. Their kindness towards us is still treasured up by me, and if ever the pleasure of meeting them again presents itself, it will be a source of happiness to shake them by the hand and thank them for past favors.

A hack was waiting in front of the office, which we got into and started for the railway which would take us to Middlesbrough.

A little while after the train had started the handcuffs were removed from our wrists. To pass the time away we amused ourselves looking out of the car windows and viewing passing objects and did all we could to make them think we did not care for being taken back to our homes; but could the secrets of our bosoms have been revealed, two aching hearts would have been discovered.

Before the train reached its destination the "bracelets" were again placed on our hands. We arrived at Middlesbrough about a quarter to 8 in the evening. Before getting out of the cars we pulled our coat sleeves over the handcuffs, and as soon as we were out in the station, we swung our hands, kept a smile on our countenances and were scarcely noticed by anyone, till we arrived at the Middlesbrough police office. No sooner had we entered the office than one of the officers in charge inquired:

"Are you the boys that have been brought back?"

I answered, "Yes."

He said, "You were not worth bringing back," which sentiment found an echo in my own heart.

CHAPTER VIII.

IN THE CELL—A VISIT FROM RICHARD'S FATHER AND MY MOTHER—THE TRIAL—THE DECISION OF THE COURT—A FEW WORDS OF EXPLANATION.

WE were soon escorted to a cell, which was much larger and colder than the one we occupied the night previous. The handcuffs taken off, the door closed upon us, and with sad hearts we sat down upon a bed of straw.

We had been in the cell but a few minutes when Richard's father came with some supper for his son. How sad he looked as he entered the cell—a father's love for his boy was clearly manifest. He did not say much, but looked hard at me, as though he blamed me for leading him from home. Of course I was a few months older than Richard, but he was taller and stouter than I, and to look at us it would hardly appear reasonable that I should have power to lead him away. Mr. Sedgwick only stayed a few moments.

The supper was soon spread. Richard, poor fellow, could not eat, but I did justice to my share. We then laid down and tried to sleep, but what with the mice and other small visitors, and thinking of our peculiar situation, we had little sleep that night, and were not sorry when daylight came.

About 8 o'clock the next morning my mother entered the cell with some breakfast for me. She did not say much but evidently felt for me. It was principally through her we had been brought back. Though one of the prime movers in our capture, she was hadrly to blame, for she believed it was her duty to do what she had done. So many tales had been told her concerning Utah and the "Mormons" that she felt positive there must be a great deal of truth in them.

About half-past 10 o'clock we were escorted into a room where an officer took a description of us—color of our hair, eyes, complexion, our height, etc. Shortly afterwards we were taken into the court room and had our trial before Judge Fallows. Besides the judge and several policemen, our employers, Richard's father and my mother were there.

The judge asked a few questions and then inquired what we had to say for ourselves. I immediately arose and said:

"What I have to say for myself is this: The room I work in is not a fit place, as it is a cold, damp cellar."

Mr. Gould denied this statement.

The judge then asked Richard what he had to say for himself. He replied that his reason for absconding was because we were such close companions, and when I ran away he followed me. One of the police said to me:

"You're the leader, then, are you?"

We were then asked by the judge whether we would serve the remainder of our apprenticeship in jail, or go back and work for our employers. We chose the latter alternative.

He then inquired of Mr. Carter what our expenses were and the amount of our passage money. On being informed, he decided that if our employers could obtain the money for our ship tickets it would clear the incurred expenses; but if not, the expenses were to be deducted out of our wages, and the case was dismissed. At this we were not sorry. I went home; but as my parents were not there I went to see Wm. H. Scott.

Before proceeding further, it may be proper to offer a few words concerning our capture. When we did not return to our homes at the time appointed, suspicion was immediately arroused and Mr. Carter told Mr. Gould and our parents he believed we were connected with the "Mormons," and had run away with the intention of going by a vessel that was to sail for America. They at once telegraphed to London to see if the ship had started and were informed it had not.

Our parents were anxious we should be brought back, and my mother begged they wou d send for us. She said she would do anything rather than have us go to Utah with the "Mormons." Mr. Gould was not much in favor of taking any steps; but Mr. Carter felt quite interested in the matter. He telegraphed to London and had a detective put on our track, and started himself for London that evening and arrived there early next morning, when, accompanied by a detective, he took us off the ship as already narrated.

To again continue the story, I spent the Saturday afternoon after our trial with Wm. H. Scott, who had not yet gone on his mission. He informed us that while we were absent he had had an unpleasant time. Both our parents and employers had suspected him of being the cause of our absconding, and not seeing him in Middlesbrough, they thought he had gone with us; but in this they were mistaken, as William, thinking they would suspect him, went to Stockton and stayed there a few days. After this interview I went home and was treated very kindly by my parents that evening.

CHAPTER IX.

A Clipping From the "Middlesbrough News"—A Promise Made but Not Fulfilled—The Second Attempt to Leave Home.

After my return home I thought seriously over the matter of absconding. I knew I had broken the law and also the promise I had made in my indentures to work seven years with Mr. Gould. Had my parents been more favorable towards me, I should not have left my home and employer to endeavor to emigrate with the Saints until I was free to act upon my own responsibility, and to do as I thought best. But now that I was back again, it was my resolve to stay and finish the remainder of my apprenticeship, providing my parents would grant me permission to attend meetings of the Saints and not be too strict with me.

As Richard and I passed along the streets, people made scornful remarks about us.

On the next Friday, June 1st, my attention was called to the following article, which appeared in the *Middlesbrough News*, published that morning:

"Saturday.—Before W. Fallows, Esq.

"Off to Mormondom.—At this court, two youths, named Richard Sedgwick and Robert Aveson, the former an apprentice with Mr. Carter of Gosford Street, and the latter with Mr. Gould of South Street, printer, were charged with absconding on the 18th ult. The lads, in company with a young man who has joined the Mormons and succeeded in converting the lads to his views, went from Sunderland and from thence to London by the steamer *Lady Havelock*, en route for Utah. A warrant was sent after them, and they were apprehended in London and brought back to Middlesbrough.—Ordered to go back to their work, and the expenses to be deducted out of their wages."

The next day, after finishing my work at 4 o'clock, Mr. Gould brought my week's wages, but instead of my usual seven shillings and sixpence he gave me five shillings and sixpence. He said he was going to deduct two shillings per week until the full amount of my expenses from London was paid. This did not meet my approval, but as it was according to the decision of the court it could not be prevented.

On the following Sunday, shortly after dinner, I told my parents I wished to go for a walk. Permission was granted, but my father accompanied me.

Richard Sedgwick's parents did not take the same course with him as my parents did with me. He could attend any meetings he wished and was permitted to go where he pleased; but a strict watch was kept over me by my mother, so that I was always in a miserable suspense. Besides this, my mother was all the time talking to me when I was at home, which made me dread to see her:

On Saturday, June 9th, my mother asked me to go with her next day to a meeting of the Wesleyan Reformers.

"Mother," I replied, "I can't serve two religions at once."

"Yours is the devil's religion!" she replied.

The next morning, on going to my trunk to get on my Sunday clothes, I discovered they were not there, and on asking my mother where they were, she said:

"Those clothes you wear every day are good enough for you to go to Mormon meetings in."

Pleased to think she would allow me to go even on those terms, I answered that it did not matter with me what kind of clothes I had on so long as the privilege was granted of attending "Mormon" meetings.

After breakfast, I went to the front door and sat on the step meditating, while people passed to and fro, dressed in their Sunday clothes. Then I looked at myself in my every-day attire, with no coat on, as mine was not to be had. It seemed to touch me on a sore part to go through the streets in my shirt sleeves, while all others were dressed in their best clothes. But I revered my religion, loved the Saints and was not going to stay in the house all day notwithstanding the clothes worn by me were shabby for the Sabbath.

The church bells were pealing and the people passing to and fro to their respective places of worship as I hurried to my place of destination—Sister Scott's—and related to the folks there how my Sunday clothes had been locked up by my mother. From one of the Saints, a young man living at Scott's, I obtained the loan of a coat. They asked me to come to the afternoon meeting, to be held at their house, which I promised to do.

Returning home about noon, my father commanded that I should stay in the house the remainder of the day. So I was prevented keeping my promise.

That afternoon was one of the most unpleasant of my life. Oh, how slowly the time passed away! I retired early to rest. My prayers were not forgotten; and while on my knees big tears rolled down my cheeks.

Richard and I intended to make our second attempt to leave home; but prior to doing so awaited an answer to a letter which had been sent to President George J. Linford while in the Thames Police office, containing our ship tickets. But three weeks passed away before the expected answer came.

On Saturday evening, June 16th, we received a letter from President Linford. It informed us that our tickets had been received all right and contained his advice to us not to again run away from our homes, but serve out our lawful apprenticeship.

The next day was the time fixed to leave our homes the second time. We intended to start at 5 o'clock in the afternoon by steamer for Shields, a town probably between forty or fifty miles northward.

In the morning of that day I attended the Presbyterian church, and it seemed to me my mother was beginning to think I was weaning myself from "Mormonism."

In the afternoon, Richard and I went to Sister Scott's. There we met some of her relatives from Shields. One of them, a young lady, not intending to return that day, gave me her ticket.

One or two acquaintances of Sister Scott were going to Shields, and we intended, on arriving there, to stay with them that night. Where our final destination would be we hardly knew, though we had been thinking of going to some part of Scotland. Richard had about £1.2s. ($5.50). I had no money, but had borrowed 5s. ($1.25) from Sister Scott.

About half past 4 o'clock we went down to a boat landing, accompanied by nearly all of the Scott family and visiting relatives, who were going to Shields. The steamer we intended to go by was timed to leave at 5 o'clock; a steamer for Stockton also started at the same time. Both the steamers were moored near each other. We were there a few minutes before 5 o'clock and went with our friends into a waiting room on the landing stage. Passengers were walking about the landing, awaiting the departure of the steamers. It was our intention to go aboard the Shields steamer; but before doing so we noticed a man named Brooks, a printer, going on the Stockton steamer. Being acquainted with him, we deemed it advisable to wait till the Stockton steamer should start, for fear Brooks would see us going on the other steamer. This placed us in a rather precarious situation, as both steamers having to start at the same time, we were afraid of being unable to get on the vessel without his seeing us. Anxiously we watched the two boats, wondering which would start first, when we saw the Stockton boat make the first move. How pleased we were! It had not got many feet away when, turning to Richard, I said quickly:

"Now, let us go!" (meaning, of course, for us to go on the Shield's steamer.)

No sooner had I spoken these words than a brother in the Church, named John Parish, hurriedly approached us and in a half whisper, said:

"*Here's your mother!*"

These words perplexed and astounded me. Was it a reality that we were stopped the second time in our attempt to leave home? To be positive that Parish was correct in his assertion I looked in the direction he pointed, and there, sure enough, was my mother gazing intently at the two steamers—one on its journey and the other just ready to start.

CHAPTER X.

PLANNING TO LEAVE HOME A THIRD TIME—LEAVE MIDDLESBROUGH—ARRIVAL AT NEWCASTLE—LEITH, EDINBURGH AND GLASGOW—A PECULIAR SITUATION: NO MONEY, NO FRIENDS—MAKE UP MY MIND TO GO TO NEW YORK—ARRIVAL AT LIVERPOOL.

I LEFT the waiting room and returned home with my mother.

It was my usual habit to be at home at 4 o'clock on Sundays, but being absent at that time on this occasion, my mother, thinking it probable I was going to a Latter-day Saint evening meeting at Stockton by steamer, came to the boat landing to look for me.

The next morning my mind was fully set to make a third attempt to leave home.

At dinner time, seeing Richard a little ahead of me on the street, I quickly overtook him and said:

"Now, Richard, make up your mind to go away to-night."

He was surprised, and said:

"We have been stopped twice now, and I don't think it's right for us to go away again; but I'll go with you if you want me to."

We then arranged to meet at the theatre, which was near a boat landing, at 7:30 that evening; he agreeing to bring with him out of my box (which was at Sister Scott's), a tin cup, some writing paper, envelopes, and pen and ink.

The working hours in the printing office were from 8 a.m. till 7:30 p.m. The train by which I intended to leave had to start at 7:45 p.m.

Shortly after 7 o'clock that evening it began to rain. The suit I wore was very thin and I would soon be wet through. I discovered also that a new pocket knife, recently purchased, had been left behind; so, thinking of the rain, my poor clothes and the knife, I was in two minds whether to go that night or not. I walked up and down the room in which I worked, hardly knowing what to do. Twenty-five minutes past seven came, but I was still undecided in my mind.

Presently I left the place and hurried down to where Richard was waiting near the theatre. He had the things which he was told to bring. Borrowing twelve shillings from him and, with the five shillings loaned me by Sister Scott, my total stock of cash was seventeen shillings.

The rain still continued and my clothes were wet. I parted with my friend Richard and went on a small steamboat which crossed the river Tees. After crossing, I purchased a ticket to Newcastle-on-Tyne for three shillings and a penny and soon boarded the cars and started on my journey.

Newcastle was reached about half past 10 o'clock that night. Getting out of the cars I looked around for a few moments at the elegant and spacious railway station and began to wonder what was the next thing to do, as it was my intention to go to Leith next morning. After finding out where the Leith steamer sailed from I procured lodgings at a private boarding house.

At 4 o'clock I was aroused and quickly dressing myself, left the house and walked the streets for nearly two long hours. About 6 o'clock the steamer started. We arrived at Leith about 5 o'clock in the evening. Among the passengers whose acquaintance I made was an Irishman, bound for Glasgow; and having the address of the president of the Glasgow Conference, I thought it would be best to go there.

We walked from Leith to Edinburgh, about two miles distant, and then took train for Glasgow, reaching the latter place about 8 o'clock. The address I wanted to go to was about two miles from the station.

After entering the house I related to the lady there the particulars of my leaving home, during which time she prepared supper for me. She told me she expected Bro. Cluff in soon. Nearly an hour afterward Brother Cluff came in. They then held a consultation regarding me and Brother Cluff said I could stay there that night, but they wished me to leave in the morning.

Next morning I started out to seek work—called at printing offices, paint shops and other places; but after traveling about all day met with no success.

In the evening I wended my way to the Conference House where they allowed me to sleep that night.

Next morning I started out again in search of employment. It appeared strange there should be numerous advertisements for boys wanted in many stores, but whenever I applied they always made some excuse.

For two long days I had tramped the streets, applying at stores of various kinds; I was anxious and willing to work but could not obtain any. All the money I had borrowed was spent—every cent—for traveling expenses, food, etc. And here was I in a strange country, without home or friends, and worst of all, no money. What was I to do? My situation was a trying one: I had left home, friends and employer, thinking to easily obtain employment and earn enough, with that deposited with the Perpetual Emigration Fund to emigrate next year to the frontier.

In the evening I returned as usual to the Conference House, feeling somewhat low-spirited, but doing my best to cheer myself up and look at the bright side.

Conversing with Brother Cluff he asked me why I did not go to New York. I replied that I might as well stay in Glasgow, because if I went there, I should not arrive in time to go with the Saints on the cars to Wyoming, the last ship having left three weeks previous.

Brother Cluff informed me that another ship had left Liverpool—the *St. Mark*—and if I took passage by steamer from Glasgow the next Saturday, I could get there before the company arrived; and said he thought it would be likely I should have a chance to go with the Saints to the frontier.

Immediately making up my mind to do as Brother Cluff had advised me, I wrote to Brigham Young, Jr., at Liverpool, asking for my money in the P. E. Fund; also to Sister Scott, telling her of my resolve.

On the Saturday morning the postman brought two letters, one of which was from Liverpool and contained a post office order,

Being too late to secure a berth on the steamer which was to leave Glasgow that morning, as all the berths were taken, I decided to take the steamer for Liverpool, which would leave that evening at 6 o'clock, and sail from there to New York. I purchased several articles of clothing, and one of the Saints in the Glasgow branch gave me a hat, shirt, muffler, etc.

In the evening, at 6 o'clock, I left Glasgow for Liverpool, which place we reached late in the afternoon of the next day. I at once proceeded to Brigham Young's office. There Elder Orson Pratt received me very kindly and asked one of the clerks to take me to a lodging house, which he did.

The steamer *Virginia* was advertised to sail for New York the following Wednesday, June 27th, and I made arrangements to embark on that vessel.

CHAPTER XI.

Arrival at Queenstown—In Suspense—"It's only a Runaway Boy They're After"—Arrival at New York—A Proposition Accepted.

Queenstown was reached the next day, June 28th. A small steamer brought us some Irish passengers, also some officers in search of some one. I felt somewhat nervous on seeing them and wondered who they were after. Who did they want? was it me? Being anxious to ascertain, I inquired of an Irishwoman who was near me:

"What do these men want?"

The answer she made surprised me.

"It's only a runaway boy they're after."

I was thunderstruck at these words, but still kept my eye on the officers. At last, seeing them make their way in the direction where I was, if it were possible for me to have sunk into the cabin, I should certainly have done so. Could I hide? No, there was no time for that.

As they approached near me I sat down, folded my arms and said to myself: "Take me if you will!" Oh, how my heart beat! Another moment and they passed by. How thankful 1 felt it was not me they were after! It transpired afterwards it was a soldier—a deserter—they were in search of.

In a very little time we were sailing on the "deep blue sea."

We arrived at New York, July 13th, being sixteen days on cur voyage.

Two or three hours after arriving I started to find out Mr. Thomas Taylor's office and was kindly invited in. No time was lost by me in accepting the invitation, as the heat was oppressive. I felt the effects very much, for no sooner was I seated than faintness overcame me. Some cold water and a fan were brought me and I soon recovered. H. P. Folsom, T. B. H. Stenhouse and others were present. Brother Folsom was formerly traveling Elder in the Durham and Newcastle Conference, and I formed his acquaintance at Middlesbrough.

After being in the office a few minutes, Brother Folsom asked me if I was from Middlesbrough, to which I answered in the affirmative. Knowing I had worked in a printing office, Brother Folsom spoke a good word for me to Brother S enhouse, editor and proprietor of the *Salt Lake Daily Telegraph*, who asked me how long 1 would work for him if he paid the remainder of my fare to the frontier. I responded two years. He then said:

"I'll make a proposition to you, Robert: I'll give you twelve dollars a week for the first year and fifteen for the second."

This proposition was eagerly accepted by me.

CHAPTER XII.

Leave New York—Arrival at Wyoming—Incidents on the Plains.

I SLEPT that night in the office. The next day Brother H. P. Folsom procured lodgings for me at Sister Mary I. Worthington's, in Brooklyn, with whom I stayed till the next Tuesday, the 17th of June, when, in company with her and her family, we left New York about midnight.

Our company consisted of about seven hundred Scandinavians (a ship having arrived on the 17th) and about one hundred English.

On the 29th of July, about noon, we arrived at Wyoming, a small settlement in Nebraska Territory. At a short distance the tents of the Saints attracted my attention, and I soon wended my way there, finding quite a number of those who had sailed in the *American Congress*. We were pleased to greet each other.

After dinner I took a stroll over to one of the stores in the settlement, where I assisted in serving customers and was given my board as a recompense.

Early in the afternoon of August 2nd, we started on our long journey. Our train consisted of about sixty-five wagons. The captain's name was Rawlings, and Brother John Nicholson was chaplain.

About twenty miles was an average day's journey. The emigrants walked most of the way, riding only in the wagons at intervals to rest themselves. Each morning, before sunrise, we were aroused by the sound of the bugle. Then could be witnessed a scene of activity; all were bustling around, some going for wood, others carrying water and lighting fires.

While camping at night, after supper had been prepared and disposed of, we enjoyed good times, especially in listening to singing, in which some young ladies excelled. Groups of elder ones could have been seen seated around large fires, conversing about days gone by and forecasting the future.

Following are some incidents which happened on the plains:

Reaching the North Platte River, and after being camped there two or three hours, one of our company appeared with two loaded guns, one of which he hurriedly handed to a young man. We asked what was the matter. He replied:

"We are surrounded by Indians!"

I then rushed to our wagon to get a pistol which I thought our teamster had left in the wagon, but could not find it. All the men left camp to ascertain what was going on. Women and children began to cry and the scene was heartrending. Those of us left in camp were eagerly looking around, expecting every minute to be attacked by Indians. Our camping place was in a lonely spot. On one side, close to us, was the North Platte River, and on the other, about the same distance, were mountains. Not a house in sight; in fact, we were a great many miles away from one. We afterwards learned that the alarm was a false one. The captain called the company together and chided the men for leaving the camp without anyone to defend it.

One snowy morning, when probably about a hundred miles from Salt Lake City, I started out, as usual, on foot. My shoes were considerably worn out, and one of them was badly used up and so hurt me that, despite the snow, I had to throw it away and walk barefoot. Approaching our teamster, I besought him to let me ride, telling him my deplorable condition. He refused to grant my request. After walking awhile I again asked permission to ride, but was again denied. The snow came down in heavy flakes and very few of our company were walking. I trudged along for about three miles with only one shoe on, when my strength failed—I could go no farther—and was about to sit down in the snow, at the same time fervently praying to my Heavenly Father for His divine assistance. As soon as I had uttered my prayer a shoe came flying out to me. Our wagon was just passing by and Sister Worthington was the person who threw it. It was small for me, but with difficulty, after rubbing some skin off my heel, I managed to get it on and went limping on my journey.

CHAPTER XIII.

Arrival in the "City of the Saints"—Keeping "Bach" —My Parents Join the Church—They Emigrate to Utah.

After a long, weary and tedious journey of about seven thousand miles, Salt Lake City was at length reached on September 30, 1866—a little over three months' travel from Liverpool to Salt Lake City. It was Sunday when we arrived. That morning I arose early, and getting something to eat, left the camp (a few miles up Parley's Canyon), and wended my way to the "City of the Saints," to find the residence of Brother T. B. H. Stenhouse. It was a fine, sunny morning; everything around me looked charming and lovely.

Onward to the heart of the city I went. After many inquiries the residence of Brother Stenhouse was at length reached. He was pleased to see me and invited me to take dinner with himself and family. In the afternoon his son, Lorenzo, took me to his father's printing office, which was my sleeping place that night.

Next morning I went to the Tithing Office yard, where our train was camped (it having arrived there that morning). President Young came into the yard to see us. He shook hands with many of the brethren and sisters, and they felt quite honored. I was informed that a number of the Saints who sailed on the *American Congress* had only arrived in the city a day or two previous. Although it was over five weeks after the departure of the *American Congress* before my leaving England. I did not lose much time after all.

I removed what little luggage I had to the *Daily Telegraph* office, thinking it best to "keep bach" for the present, as I had no relatives or any particular friend to board me. This I did for nearly eleven weeks, when, December 19, 1866, James McKnight, an employe in the *Daily Telegraph* office, told me that if it suited me I could live with him. His offer was gladly accepted and I stayed with him for several months.

During this time letters regularly reached me from my parents and I was prompt in answering them; giving full particulars about Salt Lake City and our religion, and often bore my testimony to them. I was here in Utah without a relative and was very desirous they should receive the gospel, although the prospects were not encouraging at that time.

In August, 1868, Wm. H. Scott arrived from New York (the Scott family having emigrated to New York in 1867). I was greatly pleased to meet my friend. He was the first intimate acquaintance from Middlesbrough I had seen since coming to Utah.

It is painful, however, to relate that he apostatized in the Summer of 1869. It was about the time when the "Godbeite" movement took place. From the time Brother Scott embraced the gospel he was one of the most zealous workers in the cause of truth ever seen by me. He labored faithfully to assist in establishing the latter-day kingdom; but his expectations in regard to Utah and her people were not realized. I had been very fond of him—had loved him as a brother. He had been a friend and counselor to me in past days, and when I saw that he was as much in opposition to the kingdom of God as he had been formerly in favor of building it up, it grieved me very much. I talked and reasoned with him and tried to show him the error of his way, but it was all in vain. He became more and more bitterly opposed to the gospel and in the Summer of 1870 went back to the States.

Correspondence with my parents and also my relatives was regularly kept up from the time of my arrival in Utah. I was very anxious to induce them to join the Church, and did all in my power to induce them to do so.

In the Spring of 1879, I procured the address of the president of the Middlesbrough Branch—William Garbett—and wrote to him, requesting that he should see my parents and use his best endeavors to induce them to embrace the gospel. Brother Garbett and other Saints visited with that object in view.

On the 20th of September, 1879, I was happily surprised and astonished to receive a letter from my mother with the following glad tidings:

"I, your mother, was baptized a member of the Church of Jesus Christ of Latter-day Saints, on the 23rd of August, and your father on the 30th of the same month."

This was very gratifying news, both to myself and wife. After waiting patiently and anxiously for over thirteen years, my prayers, which were so often offered up, were answered.

My reply to this letter from my parents informed them how my heart rejoiced to hear the good news, and stated that we would assist them to emigrate to Utah the following year.

The time drew nigh for my parents to arrive in Zion. After such a lengthy absence from them, and knowing how opposed to the work they had been, but now their eyes were opened and they could see as I saw, I looked forward with pleasure to the day of their arrival.

They took passage with the first company, April 10th, 1880. I almost counted the days for their arrival. At last it was announced by telegram that the company would arrive at 6:30, p.m., April 30, 1880. Every preparation was made by us for their comfort.

CHAPTER XIV.

My Parents in Zion—Arrival of Richard Sedgwick in Salt Lake City—His Story of Leaving Home in 1867—How the President of the Middlesbrough Branch was Emigrated—Re-union of the Middlesbrough Branch.

The next morning they were enabled to get a better view of he "City of the Saints." It was the first of May—a fine sunny day. The orchards were delightful for the eye to gaze upon; the peach, plum, apple, and other trees were arrayed in their sweetest attire. The birds were merry, the bee and butterfly passed too and fro, and everything around was beautiful.

My parents were much in love with our city and the surroundings. During the day father was seen to shed tears—tears of joy and sorrow. He was glad he was here in the land of Zion, but felt sorrowful to think of his sons and daughter in Babylon. To a neighbor who happened to be near him, and saw the tears roll down his cheeks, he said he felt sorry to think that his children back in England were so foolish to stay there, when they might have been here in this beautiful country.

My parents have often expressed, that they wished they had come here years ago.

About the latter part of October, 1880, I was much pleased to receive a letter from my brother Miles, at Middlesbrough, stating that he had been baptized into the Church.

In September, 1881, I sent his fare to emigrate him to Utah, and he arrived in Salt Lake City, Nov. 11th.

My readers no doubt, have been wondering what became of Richard Sedgwick. When I bade him good-by in England, I little thought so many years would elapse before we should meet again. After my leaving Middlesbrough, he stayed there a little over one year, then emigrated to New York and resided in Brooklyn, at which place he was married in July, 1868. Our correspondence continued more or less, from the time he reached that place till he arrived in the valleys of the mountains, November 10, 1882. When we met I should not have known him, nor would he have recognized me, had I not answered to my name when he inquired for me. It was nearly sixteen years and a half since we saw each other, and it was a happy meeting.

The following is Richard Sedgwick's account of his leaving home in 1867:

"I started from home on the 1st of July, 1867. It was on a Monday morning, and on Mondays we used to commence work at 8 o'clock, while other mornings, we began at 6. I took the train for Stockton (four miles away), and on arriving there called at the house of Brother Thomas Watson, clerk of the Middlesbrough and Stockton branch. The box, which we had with us when we left our homes the year previous, was at Brother Watson's house. I told him I wanted it, as it was my intention to go to Liverpool, and from there to New York. Brother Watson was not in favor of my going away, and advised me to return home, but my mind was bent on leaving for New York and then get to Utah as soon as possible. He kept talking with me till I missed the train for Liverpool. This was unpleasant, as I was afraid Mr. Carter would send an officer after me.

"Determined not to be baffled, I took my box, went to the station and waited for the next train, perhaps two hours, and arrived at Liverpool about 2 o'clock in the afternoon. It so happened that a steamer had to leave for New York early next morning. I went to 42 Islington, and got my passage money which I had paid to sail on the *American Congress* the year previous.

"Next morning I was up bright and early and went aboard the steamer. The vessel sailed about half-past 9 o'clock, and it was well she started at that hour, for I learned afterwards, by letter from my father, that as soon as Carter missed me, he lost no time in trying to have me brought back again. A detective was put on my track, who, fortunately for me, arrived at the Liverpool docks just a few hours too late."

On September 12, 1881, I received a letter from William Garbett, president of the Middlesbrough branch, which stated in effect that there had been a death in his family, another reduction in wages, a poor harvest on account of incessant rains, and provisions were rising in price. In answer, I told him my faith was that he would be emigrated to Utah before the end of the next year. Circulars were issued by me to his friends, explaining his situation. The result was sufficient means were procured to emigrate Brother Garbett and family (seven in number) to Utah. They arrived here in Sept., 1882.

Reflecting at various times on the scenes recounted in this little work, and of the many joyful times experienced among the Saints in Middlesbrough and vicinity, it occurred to the writer that a revival of old times and acquaintanceships would be greatly relished by those who had emigrated therefrom, and it was finally arranged to have a re-union of the Middlesbrough branch of the church on Thanksgiving day, November 29, 1883.

All the Saints and Elders who had been in the branch were invited to be present at the 4th Ward meeting house, where the re union was held. Dinner was served at 2 p. m., followed by the various exercises, such as singing, reciting, speaking, etc. The time was agreeably spent till half-past 6 o'clock in the evening. The attendance was numerous without being crowded, and the affair was gratifying to all present. It will remain indelibly impressed upon the memories of all who participated.

A BOY'S LOVE: A MAN'S DEVOTION.

CHAPTER 1.

WILLIAM ANDERSON'S HEART AND HAND—HIS EARLY LIFE, HOME AND SURROUNDINGS.

TWO little shreds of yellow paper which would not pass current for the value of an ordinary letter stamp! And yet they are to be cherished in the family Bible as a treasure worthy of loving gaze and reverent touch.

Look at them closer. One resembles a hand and the other a heart. Even in their freshest and brightest days they would have been condemned by the artist whose standard is the ideal, and by the anatomist whose sole appreciation is for the real; for their departure from anatomical truth is not in the line of artistic license. Still they are sacred to us.

Why are the papers so yellow? you ask. Because more than half a century has elapsed since they were cut into these shapes. Why so frayed and worn? Because for years they were carried in a woman's bosom. Why so stained? Because they have been wept over; and doubtless some of the bitterest of all tears—the tears which fall from the widowed and the fatherless, have moistened them. But here is a deeper stain than any which can be made by any human tears—what is it? The blood of an honest man, a patriot; the blood which flowed from the real heart of the man whose real hand clipped these little uncouth models from the old-fashioned sheet and sent them to his lady-love.

Turn the papers over. What do you read?

"William Anderson sends this hand to his sweetheart, Emeline T. Stewart. Like myself, it is yours now and forever, if you will it so.

"NEW VINEYARD, MAINE, Christmas, 1829."

"Dear Emeline:
I offer my heart to you. Keep it if you can love me and will be my wife.

"Your true lover—and husband, as I hope to be,
WILLIAM ANDERSON."

The writing is cramped, for the hand which laboriously traced so many words within so small a space, though it belonged to the young schoolmaster of the village, was quite as well used to carrying a rifle or wielding an ax in the forest as to this scholar's work. The composition, too, is heavy: William Anderson was not a poet; he was but a plain youth whose best effort was to put his honest wish into honest words, and to send his blunt message freighted with all his hopes for the future.

Little did he know how his paper hand and heart would be hoarded to come into the loving care of his descendants! The strong man is dead—his mangled clay rests amid the decaying beauties of a city by the banks of the lordly Mississippi. The devoted woman is dead—her tortured body reposes under mighty Wahsatch shadows. But the fragile papers survive; and the love which brought them into being lives. It lives eternally, if there be reward in heaven for sacrifice.

William Anderson was the son of a New Vineyard farmer —well to do with the grosser goods of this world, as well as being possessed of family pride; and the boy was taught, along with the heavy duties of the field, something of books. He was indulged, too, in the physical luxury of a yearly meeting-suit, made out of wondrous fabrics brought all the way from Boston, a city more distant and mythical in the estimation of the New Vineyard people of that day than is Benares to this age.

Large families of children were in the sturdy and healthy New England fashion of the first quarter of this century, and William's brothers and sisters numbered near a half score. So the boys were impelled to industry and self-reliance.

Religious profession of some kind was one of the common comforts of life; and Mrs. Joy Anderson was proud to marshal "for meetin'" each Sabbath a troop as numerous and well-behaved as the family party of Charity Carver or Hope Smith. William's mother was of a Puritan family, and vied with her female neighbors, whose names indicated the same proud descent, in having every able member of her household a regular attendant upon divine service.

From the country within a radius of five miles of the plain, old-fashioned, stone meeting house, came, for gossip as much as genuine worship, all the settlers—rich and poor, farmers, graziers, woodsmen and the few traffickers who were able to make their Yankee shrewdness a means of maintenance.

One of the principal men of the region comprised in the scattered village of New Vineyard, was Hugh Stewart, farmer and whilom speculator in lands and timber. His family was wont to journey from his residence to the church—a distance of two miles in a carryall.

This vehicle was the object of much reverence; and Hugh managed by frequent applications of varnish to keep it in that state of glossiness which constituted its chief awe in New Vineyard eyes. Regularly, rain or shine, its appearance at the last turn of the sandy road leading to the meeting-house was announced by some watchful youngster and the waiting worshipers, who usually assembled an hour in advance of sermon time, rushed to the porch to watch the family of the Stewarts dismount from their carriage. Though this practice was continued for a term of years, it never failed to awaken interest. I doubt if the London Lord Mayor's gilded chariot ever aroused more real excitement among his satiated townsmen than was evinced at each appearance of this ancient vehicle at the meeting-house steps.

The occupants of the carryall were invariably checked off upon a score of fingers: "There's Hugh and Martha, and there's Dan'l and Marchant and Em'line and Car'line."

If one of these usual attandants happened for any reason to be absent, there were comments and surmises without number until some active investigator could ascertain the cause; and once learned, the news was whispered about from lips quivering with eagerness to tell unto ears twitching with anxiety to hear.

One of the most intensely interested of the watchers was Mrs. Joy Anderson, who felt all that her religion would permit her to entertain of envy for the almost regal state in which the Stewarts were brought to church.

More than one scathing rebuke fell from her very capable tongue upon the well-calloused understanding of William, the senior Anderson. Her stock complaint is worthy of preservation as showing how little the style of marital reproach has varied within three-quarters of a century.

"I don't care for myself, and you know I don't; I don't say a grumbling word at you for not taking me to New York when Mrs. Stewart went with her husband though you know well enough you were quite as able to pay my way as he was to take his wife; and everybody knows that if anyone deserves a rest I do; but no, I never can go to visit my cousin Faith Brewster that I think the world of, though I've never seen her and only heard from her twice in my life, and she may have been dead these ten years for all I know or you care, and even then it would only be my duty to visit her grave and I could carry along a little box of mignonette, in case of, to plant on her last resting place—no I never say one word about these things, and I always spare your feelings instead of telling you how often Mrs. Stewart looks at me as if she had a kind of contemptuous pity for my suffering; but what I feel so awfully hurt about are the airs that the Stewart children put on when they get out of the carriage on Sunday at the meeting-house door; and we've got more than half the distance to travel and you could well afford something of the kind, and then we could get to the meeting-house even if some of us were sick, and because we've had not a day's sickness in the house in fifteen years is no sign we won't have, but all the more sign that it must come sooner or later——"

Though this somewhat inconsistent speech was received with no apparent emotion by the substantial husband and father whom it was intended to pierce with its sharp sarcasm; it always created a little excitement among the children.

Mrs. Stewart was really a good woman who was compelled by frequent attacks of illness to pay some attention to personal comfort, and who had never thought of triumphing over her esteemed friend Joy with a glance of pity. Mrs. Anderson was also a good woman; but she unwittingly taught her children to hold envy and dislike for neighbors. Probably she was not the first woman, as she was certainly not the last to pursue this foolish, unchristianlike course.

Little William was often an attentive listener to this wail of his mother; and from it he tried to conceive a deep and bitter hatred for the rival aristocratic family at the other end of the village.

Very strangely, this effort of the boy, begun and religiously pursued under a sense of family loyalty, was utterly unavailing. There was something in the soft eyes and patient face of Mrs. Stewart which consumed all his bitter thoughts and made him feel more like kissing the lady's hand than hating her, even for his injured mother's sake.

Often and often when she was assisting the children from the carriage, while Hugh—something too careless in this respect, was taking his horse from the thills or hailing neighbors in a hearty voice, little Will Anderson felt a barely resistible inclination to rush forward and offer his help. Was he restrained by a fear of punishment from his mother, or the cule from the assembled villagers? Not one of these fears influenced him in the least: he was simply afraid that there was one of the children that he could not lift. It was not tall Dan, nor fat March; for he felt that he could toss them both over the meeting house if such conduct would have been advantageous to the Stewart family; though either of the boys was as large as two such chaps as Will. And of course it was not little Carrie, for she was only a baby, three years old, "lighter than goose down," as Will thought, but did not say aloud. But it was Emeline.

Will had looked this girl in the face, from a distance, two or three times—she had brown eyes, deep and true; and brown hair, in heavy, rich coils. Her face was as full of unsullied beauty as a lily blossom. It had always a thoughtful expression as if the little brain were solving some grave problem of more than human interest. At least, all this is what Will saw and felt in an indistinct sort of fashion. I doubt if she were quite so ethereally beautiful as Will imagined; for girls born and reared on New England farms are not as fragile as a hot-house flower, and I dare say that she laughed as often as other girls; I know from personal knowledge that in later life she was not too prim to play practical jokes.

But Will felt that he could not, for his very life, offer to lift this girl from the carriage step. He was stout and heavy twelve years old; and Emeline was light and slender nine; yet the exertion, especially if she should happen to look at him from her wonderful eyes, would be fatal.

CHAPTER II.

BOYHOOD SPORTS—AN AMATEUR MILITIA—A CAMPAIGN INCIDENT—WILL ANDERSON'S GALLANTRY—CHRISTMAS MORNING GREETING—THE AFTERNOON SERVICE—A COMBAT AMONG THE BOYS.

WILL was more than five years old when peace was declared after the second war with Great Britain; and the subject, in that time of slow-moving news, was still a matter for frequent talk when he completed his tenth year. He was then admitted into the ranks of the "Continental Veterans," an organization of the patriotic youths who trained along the roads and in the woods adjoining the village, and told to each other, with passionate interest, all the tales of adventure and heroism which they could glean from their elders. The youngsters kept up really an accurate show of a military organization; including this important feature (which they had learned from the example of their elders), that all were officers of some rank or other. In the day-time they built fires in the woods on the banks of the Penobscot; and pretended that they were surrounded by night, dark as a stack of black cats. Occasionally they captured a calf and tried it as a spy by court-martial; usually allowing it to escape, at the last moment, its sentence of hanging, and then putting the guards on trial for aiding in the escape.

Four years of this training made Will a major, all the elder boys ranking from lieutenant colonel upward.

One afternoon late in the Autumn, when they were having a jolly good time in ambush along the old south road, a picket sentry announced a body of the enemy advancing rapidly. The hostile party consisted of one little girl, Emeline Stewart, who was trotting briskly homeward from her weekly visit to the village sewing school. Will was scouting at another point in company with Emeline's two brothers; and when one of the colonels suggested taking the entire force of the enemy prisoner of war, no dissenting voice was raised.

They met and seized her, poor, timid, little Emeline! She knew these boys, her school-fellows and playmates, and they were not rough; but they kept up such a style of martial bravado, and talked so glibly of court-martial and execution—they rehearsed with such sanguinary details the precedents established last week by the hanging of eight Hessian and Tory spies, that the child was struck speechless with fear.

From long practice, the young rogues acted with as much confidence and presence of mind as if they had been really old soldiers. What alarmed Emeline most of all was that they never once lapsed back from soldiers into the village boys of her acquaintance. Look at them with pleading eyes as much as she would, they gave no response. Without knowing how they were startling the child, the boys kept on with their cruel work.

A council of war was called, with General Hezekiah Bradford presiding; and before this pompous assemblage Emeline was commanded to stand and plead. She burst into tears and then sank down upon the mossy sward, while the boys, struck with sudden remorse, gazed blankly at her and then at each other.

At this instant Will and his companions hurried into the camp. A few words of explanation from one of Will's brothers revealed the whole situation, including the identity of "the enemy."

While they were gazing at the child's recumbent form, Hezzy Bradford spoke:

"Guards, remove the prisoner, and"——

He was about to conclude with "set her at liberty;" but Will did not wait to hear the conclusion. Deeming this speech but a continuation of the cruelty shown toward Emeline, he rushed at the president of the court-martial and with one accidentally-directed bunt, he knocked that august official from his seat of pine boughs and sprawled him upon his back, breathless and helpless for the moment.

Without waiting for any consultation or help, Will picked up the slender child and darted away with her; while the Continental Veterans, including Emeline's brothers, stood gaping as if they had lost their senses.

Once out upon the road and far enough from the camp to show that immediate pursuit was not intended, Will was fain to place Emeline upon a bank, that they both might get breath.

The child looked at him with wonder, at first mingled with fear. But soon she realized that he was her rescuer and began to thank him in her tender, cooing way; soon changing to a just and fiery indignation at her tormentors.

Will's physical exertion had been a trifle compared with the overwhelming nature of Emeline's glance. He was now ready to wilt. He might have fled ignominiously, but just at that moment when he felt himself about to take this course a shout came from the boys in the wood.

Will at once squared himself sturdily, intending to encounter all comers. But Emeline, with a cry of affright, sprang to her feet and cried:

"Oh, quick, Will! Let us run for home or those wicked boys will catch me again!"

At this familiar invitation, the boy took the outstretched hand of the child into his own broader palm; and thus together they ran toward the Stewart residence, Will giving the little girl a helpful lift at every step of the flight.

Looking back as they ran, Will saw his comrades emerge from the wood and shake their warrior fists at the fugitives; but he readily observed that a hopeful pursuit was deemed out of the question, and that the boys were not intending to chase.

The gate opening into the Stewart grounds was speedily reached and then Will stopped and expected Emeline to enter. But she remained outside long enough to say:

"Will Anderson, you are better than a brother to me. If you had not been there, so good and brave, what could I have done!"

When the grateful child at last disappeared within the house, Will turned to walk slowly back to the village.

turn of the road leading through the wood. Raising his eyes at some slight sound in front, he saw a phalanx of the Continental Veterans drawn up in line across his path; while at the same moment a similar body of troops closed in from the sides and took position a few steps in the rear of his person. Will was taken in an ambuscade, which was performed so successfully and with such perfect regard to military precedent, that it is probably talked of to this day in New Vineyard among the great grandchildren of the Continental Veterans.

A colonel solemnly placed Will under arrest; and then, by command of General Bradford, the troop marched to the encampment in the depths of the pine wood.

The court-martial so abruptly dismissed an hour before was now ceremoniously re-convened, and William Anderson, major in the Continental Veterans, was charged with an attack upon his superior officer. The accusation was proved and the sentence of the court, General Bradford still sitting as presiding officer, was that the culprit be dismissed the service.

As the sentence was being pronounced, Will sprang to his feet and shouted:

"Boys, don't carry this any further. I believe in military discipline, but let us settle this matter outside of the army.

"Hezzy, if I hit you, I did it accidentally; but I'm ready to take the consequences, and I'll stand up and fight you until you get satisfaction. Come on, you're bigger than I am and you're three years older; you're sure to get the best of it. Let's fight it out between us two and let that settle the matter."

Such a plan did not entirely suit the general. He remarked:

"You're sentenced; and you'll have to quit the service. But I'll give you plenty of 'consequences' besides, so make ready."

This truthful historian grieves to say that in the fight which ensued, General Bradford disgraced his uniform by cowardice; that most of the boys were afraid to interfere even when they saw the plainest rules of combat violated by the strapping

To Will's credit be it said that he fought with all the energy of his being, administering occasional terrific blows on the rosy nose of the general; and that he made no cry for quarter even when soundly thrashed.

After the encounter, the boys dispersed to their homes.

Will's heart was full of grief—not so much for the licking as for his dismissal from the ranks of the Continental Veterans. But he tried to bear up bravely in the hope that Emeline's kind feeling for him was permanent and not dependent upon his military position.

The Stewart boys went home with some shame in their minds for the unsoldier-like part which they had played in the thrilling events of the afternoon. But they sought to make amends by describing Will's chivalry and pluck in most extravagant terms to Emeline and all the other younger members of the household.

Emeline was deeply interested in the recital; and her soft little heart was torn between reverence for Will's heroism and indignation at the baseness of his persecutors—even her own brothers coming in for a lecture which made them hang their heads and look at each other in a most woe-begone fashion.

During the next few days Will had much to suffer; for big boys who were high officers in the Vets. laughed at him, and little boys, whose highest temporary aspiration was to belong to that corps, sneered and chuckled whenever they caught sight of this dismounted "knight of the sorrowful visage."

Seven weeks passed before Christmas morning dawned in that bitterly cold Winter of 1823. With the rising of the sun that day, two boys drawing a sled on which was seated a little girl, well wrapped and cuddled, appeared at the door of the Anderson residence—the girl was Emeline and the boys were Dan and March, whom she had forced into reluctant service. They entered the big kitchen, upon the invitation of Mrs. Joy, and amid a chorus of salutations in which the visitors bore their part.

When they were fairly in the house, with the biting frost shut out and the tumult ended, Emeline asked for Will.

It is very unromantic but it is truth that the object of her inquiry was at that particular moment seated at one corner of the fireplace, straining himself black in the face to draw on a pair of damp cowhide boots over a pair of similarly damp woolen socks—all of which personal belongings he had been seeking to dry by the morning fire, when this astounding interruption came.

Will succeeded in getting both boots on "as far as the heels," but go no further they would; and when his father called him to come forward, the poor boy got up and walked in agony and distortion toward Emeline. He was at least three inches taller than common, from the fact that his chubby heels rested upon the high, implacable stiffening of the boots; and his face wore a twisted look of agony which, coupled with his abnormal height, would have made him unrecognizable by casual acquaintances.

Most of the family laughed, and Dan and March joined in the hilarity—for really Will did appear grotesque; but Emeline either from absolute unconsciousness or gentle cunning, did not seem to notice the boy's awkward situation, and she began to talk to him with a self-possession entirely unruffled.

"Will," she said, "I have brought you a pair of mittens for a Christmas gift. They're my first knitting and mother says they're not good enough for a present; but they're the best I can do now, and I offer them to you because you've been so kind to me and had to suffer so much for my sake. I hope you will wear them, will you?"

Emeline had ample time for this long speech. Poor Will was dumb and gulping. But before it was ended his confusion had shrunk his feet so that he was able to literally sink into his boots, and with this relief his face had changed from a purple hue to a good tint of health. He found his voice in time to answer:

"That I will, if mother will let me—that is, I mean if your mother will let me."

And so the blushing boy stretched out his hand and took the package, but Emeline kept a tight hold of one end of the cloth in which the mittens were wrapped, as she was under positive instructions from her thrifty mother to return the piece of hickory, for which the shoulder of Dan's second-best shirt was even then yawning.

The separation of the gift from its wrappings was soon achieved, and the hickory tucked into the depth of Emeline's pocket. Then wholesome maple sugar was produced, and with it a few pieces of sugar candy such as some of those young lips had never before had an opportunity to smack over. During the hilarity which ensued, Will was doing his best to creep back into a state of self-possession. But this work was prodigious and slow; for when he had several times fairly arrived at a stage of comparative comfort, a friendly glance from the kind little knitter sent him again into a state of confusion. After the Christmas luxuries had been distributed and given lodgment in capacious stomachs or economizing pockets, the Stewart children departed and left Will to the ungentle raillery of his family. Being amply able to care for himself in a family contest with either ridicule or logic as the weapon—or, what is sometimes as good as both, a downright unreasoning self-assertiveness, Will felt no pain during the assault to which he was subjected; rather, he derived keen enjoyment from it.

In the afternoon sacred services were held in the meeting house; for these people gave to every observance, which they deemed holy, their highest esteem, and nearly all the inhabitants of the village were present. Probably the good old preacher who was a new comer to the village, had delivered forty other Christmas sermons, or even the same sermon forty other times; but familiarity with the subject had not lessened his power.

He first stilled the buzz of gossiping whisper when he announced that his text would be from one of the great poets; and the congregation bent with horror to hear what dreadful thing he next would utter. Even into this remote corner of the New World had penetrated the evil fame of the irreverent poet lord, "Childe Harold," and even the very name of poet brought with it an oppressive sense of sin.

The false impression was soon removed. In a voice rendered

tremulous by age and feeling, the minister repeated some of the verses of Milton—the Christian whose earthly sight had been lost at last to make his Heavenly vision more comp'ete. As the wonderful words of adoration filled the house of wo·ship, every head was bowed in contrition for unworthy thought:

> "This is the month and this the happy morn,
> Wherein the Son of Heaven's eternal King,
> Of wedded maid and virgin mother born,
> Our great redemption from above did bring;
> For so the holy sages once did sing,
> That he our deadly forfeit should release,
> And with his Father work us a perpetual peace.

Having won his congregation to solemnity of feeling, the preacher taught them that "All good Christians celebrate the day of Christ's nativity, a day of joy both in heaven and on earth: in heaven for a day of glory unto God on 'high; on earth for a day of peace here below, and good-will towards men; a day of joy to all people past, present and to come; such a day as wherein, after long expectation, the best return was made that ever came to the poor sons of men; such a day as the Lord Himself made. Let us therefore rejoice therein!"

Even impatient and restless youth was awed by the manner and words of the earnest minister; and the boys restrained within unusual bounds their desire to be out of church amidst the hearty enjoyments of the day.

When the service was ended, the people dispersed more slowly and thoughtfully than was their wont; but humanity cannot long be kept upon such an exalted plane of feeling, and soon began the gossip and familiarity common to the occasion. Especially among the young people was the reaction quickly noticeable; and while the elders were speaking of the latest birth, death and marriage, the children were already beginning to romp even at the very door of the meeting-house. The youngsters, despite their exceptional appreciation of the sermon, and even more as a wilful revulsion from their noteworthy behavior, were determined now to compensate themselves for self-sacrifice; and they gathered in a noisy crowd in the street passing before the house of worship.

The sun was sending down his best Winter beams, and the snow was made just moist enough for sport; so a contest of snow-balling was at once informally arranged between the boys. Hezzy Bradford was one of the leaders, and when he and his rival had each made choice of two or three of the larger boys, someone already chosen said to Hezzy:

"Take Will Anderson—there he comes. He's the straightest thrower of the lot."

But Hezzy, whose dislike of Will had been steadily augmenting since the fight in the pine grove, was not ready to make peace with his victim. So he shook his head and sneeringly cried:

"Here comes the baby who wears mittens to a snow-balling match, for fear that his fingers will get wet. Watch me tip his cap off!"

With these words Hezzy threw an icy snow-ball which he had been carelessly making while choosing sides. The missile flew straight to its mark, and Will felt his head stung sharply as his cap tumbled into the road.

Will saw the hand of Hezzy and knew that retaliation meant a renewal of hostilities; but he did not hesitate. He pulled off his valued mittens, crowded them into his pockets and in a moment proved that any praise of his accurate throwing was not ill bestowed. He cast a snow-ball fairly into Hezzy's ear, rather staggering that blusterer, and causing a peal of laughter to go up from the crowd.

As our boy had expected, Hezzy declared war and rushed forward to summarily punish this reckless antagonist.

Was it that the insult to the mittens had nerved Will with a superhuman strength? or was it that all the indignation of weeks became suddenly centered in his arm? Whatever may have been the reason, he fought with an effective vigor, before which Master Hezekiah Bradford, general, village bully and aspiring sweetheart was compelled to go ingloriously down. Briefly and plainly told, Will, to his own astonishment, no less than to the marvel of the spectators, licked Hezzy until that great military commander was glad to cry for quarter and surrender unconditionally.

More than one oppressed youngster was gladdened by the result of this combat; and so great was the excitement produced that the general contest was incontinently forsaken.

Hezzy was led away by his brothers and one or two others, who gave him a kind of contemptuous attention; but the majority of the boys crowded near to the conqueror.

From this hour, Will's rank among his companions was undisputed. He had soundly thrashed the commander-in-chief of the Continental Vets.; and without any request from himself, he was speedily restored to his former rank of major, only to relinquish that position very soon to be installed in the chief place vacated, in profound disgust, by Hezekiah Bradford.

Nor was this the least of his triumphs. When next he met Mrs. Stewart she praised his powers in unstinted terms. Though the conscientious lady could not exactly approve of fighting among boys, nevertheless she felt that Will's troubles and subsequent victories were traceable directly to his manly defense of her daughter; and Mrs. Stewart could not withhold her congratulations. And Emeline, herself, from out her brown eyes looked such pleasure at him during the next school session that he felt almost self-reproachful at receiving so much reward.

CHAPTER III.

THE PROGRESS OF THE AGE—WILL ANDERSON'S COURTSHIP—THE CHRISTMAS SERMON.

In those times the months moved on in serene procession with the people of New Vineyard. In a later age of rapidly-recurring marvels we are wont to speak of the first quarter of this century as a "slow-poke, old-fogy time;" we contemptuously wonder how men endured the tedious drag of the seasons.

In William Anderson's journal I find a note which gives token of the dawn of this great modern day of progress. He writes:

"*August* 2, 1824.—Not many days ago, Mr. Stewart gave me a newspaper to read; he said something was in it which ought to interest a bright boy like myself. (I only repeat this because Emeline's father said it.) The paper is the *Hancock Gazette and Penobscot Patriot*, of May 26, 1824; and it tells of a wonderful ship which has come into the lower waters of our river. It works with fire instead of wind and it can walk against tide, or current, or gale, as well as a horse can trot against a breeze. I have heard before of this marvelous thing called a steamship, but never thought it was a true wonder; but if it is really traveling up against a heavy Penobscot current, fire or steam or something else that is unusual must move it, for I am sure that no landward breeze that ever came off the Atlantic could do such a work. At any rate, I must see this strange ship and decide whether I shall believe or not."

The biographer finds that Providence favored Will with a trip to Bangor later in the year. How he came to be thus blessed the excited youth does not relate—beyond the fact that he went with his father, who adventured so far from home as a factor of the log men of the upper Penobscot to deal with the opulent lumber-mill owners at Bangor. Much that ensued upon this important journey is lost to us, through Will's hurried state after his return. But we learn that the steamship was actually a fact; for Will stepped on board the *Maine*, a boat of one hundred tons burthen, commanded by Captain Porter—the first steamer and the first steamer captain to be in Penobscot waters. And it is also proven that the wondrous vessel could move without the aid of sails; for after Will had disembarked he saw her shift her moorings a quarter of a mile directly against wind and current.

What most fills the journal at this period is that Will was scratching an aching and unresponsive head, seeking to decide upon some suitable present for Emeline which could be compassed by the contents of his little bead purse. After much anxiety he felt a sudden thrill of satisfaction as he remembered the poet whose sublime words the old preacher had quoted last Christmas day. He found, after much search, a shoe shop where books were also kept (for in those days business was not so scrupulously and appropriately divided as now). But, alas! the only copy of Milton was priced at twenty-seven shillings, while his purse held scarcely half that much!

He turned away in utter disappointment, when the thought came to him:

"Why do I seek the modern poet who sang of Jesus? The book which tells all we know of Him, I am sure is easier got."

He retraced his steps, and upon the cobbler-bookseller's shelves he found a red morocco-bound Testament, which was offered at thirteen shillings; and this he bought and later reverently packed away among the wonderful supplies which had been purchased by the elder William under distant direction of the precise and thrifty Mrs. Joy.

It was bleak November when the two Williams Anderson returned to New Vineyard. What holiday secrets they had in store they kept well; and the Christmas Day brought many surprises.

To Emeline—found upon the Stewart mansion door-steps that sacred morning—came a little package which, unwrapped, showed a Testament bound in red morocco. That precious little book is now before the eyes of this historian. Upon its yellow-stained title page are discernible these words:

"My friend, EMELINE T. STEWART,
"You will please accept this Testament as a gift from
"Your Friend,
"WILLIAM ANDERSON.

"EMELINE:—Ask, and ye shall receive. Knock, and it shall be opened unto you."

Four years slipped away. During this time Will was bashfully loving Emeline; and Emeline, well, she was bashfully watching Will's love.

This wondrous flower of affection grows by "bashful watching" just as morning glories unfold in greeting to the hour of enchantment. And when the Christmas Day of 1828 came, each of these dear children went to church and watched the other.

The sermon was, for Christmas, a novel one, both in text and treatment. It related to marriage as a state ordained for man; and the text was from Fuller's "Holy State," wherein it is declared:

"It is the policy of the Londoners, when they send a ship into the Levant or Mediterranean Sea, to make every mariner therein a merchant, each seaman adventuring somewhat of his own, which will make him more wary to avoid, and more valiant to encounter dangers. Thus married men, especially if having posterity, are the deeper shares in the state wherein they live, which engageth their affections to the greater loyalty. And though bachelors be the strongest stakes, yet married men are the best binders in the hedge of the commonwealth."

Will's mind must have been holding a thought not utterly foreign to the text; for he unconsciously nodded approval of the very sensible sentiment; and then he glanced at Emeline. The same instant, her eyes were lifted from a strained look at the floor and were turned in his dinrectiion. One long gaze passed between them; and this was Will's informal proposition of marriage and Emeline's informal acceptance.

CHAPTER IV.

WILLIAM ANDERSON'S MARRIAGE AND JOURNEY WESTWARD—HE AND HIS WIFE HEAR THE GOSPEL—VISIT NAUVOO—GATHER WITH THE SAINTS—THE BATTLE OF NAUVOO.

It was five hours less than one year later in the serene chronology of New Vineyard, when Will sent his paper heart and hand to Emeline. His trusty younger brother, Barton, was his messenger; and to escape observation, the boy was compelled to go early and return quickly. At breakfast, Will saw Barton enter the house and one glance told that the mission had been successfully performed.

Some hours later, at the regular Christmas services in the meeting-house, Will saw Emeline. His look was an anxious question, and hers was a gentle affirmative answer; and this was Will's formal proposition of marriage and Emeline's formal acceptance.

William Anderson and Emeline T. Stewart were wedded in their little town of New Vineyard, September 6, 1831.

Is this too abrupt? It might be if marriage were the end of the story; but unlike fiction, in real life the most uneventful period of human existence is from engagement to marriage; and unlike fiction, in real life the importance of existence comes after marriage.

Not long did they remain in their little village home. For William had decided to seek a greater measure of prosperity in the wide lands lying far beyond New Vineyard in the mysterious West.

Happy indeed was the fortune which carried them away from Maine. Their long journey across half a continent was a revelation of Divinity to their souls. Mountain, forest, lake, cataract, valley—breathed with beauty and grandeur. Two ardent beings, viewing all things under the radiance of their mutual love, saw the majesty of the land, the water and the arching cloud space above, with reverent eyes—for beyond these tangible evidences of sublime power, they sensed the Eternal Cause,

It was in the days and weeks of lonely journeying that they learned how to pray; they felt that never again would supplication and song of praise to Almighty God be formal lip-service given only at stated intervals—rather it would be an hourly and often silent communion with the Creator. In the day, they felt the Holy Presence in every glory which adorned the earth; at night, in the quiet of the woods, they gazed through swaying tree-tops, and saw the stars shedding earthward a serene beauty: and they knew that the God who, from His far-off seat of power, could unfold the swamp-pink flowers by the side of their lonely path, and could send through unfathomed space the light of countless spheres to cheer the silent watches of the night—could also lend His special care to the sentient worshiping creatures of His love.

Far away upon the prairie they at last decided to make their home. They settled in Bureau County, Illinois; and William became a sturdy western farmer. In the ten years following their marriage three children came to make their domestic happiness complete. The eldest was a son, Augustus; the others were daughters, Caroline and Martha.

Each season of the year brought its allotted toil, and the reward of perseverance and thrift was earthly prosperity.

Occasionally they heard rumors of a strange sect of religious believers, with a prophet, who dwelt in a wonderful city on the banks of the Mississippi, far to the south-west of their home. And one Summer day in 1841, four strange men, plain but pleasing in appearance, stopped at their door. These men were missionaries of the Church of Jesus Christ, journeying from the city of Nauvoo to proclaim His words to the honest-in-heart throughout the land. They left their marvelous message with William and Emeline, with the admonition to pray to God who would reveal whether the doctrine was true or false; and one of them in leaving prophesied in these words:

The prophecy was fulfilled. Before many days had elapsed the truth was plain to the minds of William and Emeline; and they awaited anxiously the visit of an Elder who might give them membership in the Church of their Savior. When weeks passed without the appearance of missionaries William regretted his obduracy at the time when he was first pressed to accept the truth.

Later, another opportunity came, and on the 15th day of August of that year, 1841, in the waters of Bureau Creek, William was immersed in sacred baptism. Afterward, Emeline rendered similar reverence to the requirement of the gospel.

As soon as he could garner his crops, William felt that he must hasten to the beautiful city of the Father of Waters. He carried with him on the eventful journey to Nauvoo his wife and their three little ones; and they reached the city on Thursday, September 30th, 1841.

On the day following, the great conference of the Church was to have opened; but the storm prevented the assembling of the Saints. And after learning that the meetings were postponed for one day, William left his wife and children comfortably shielded in their wagon from the blast while he wandered about regardless of the storm. He looked with awestruck vision upon the temple which was rearing its majestic presence toward heaven; and he gazed with curiosity at the place which was being excavated for the foundation of the Nauvoo House.

The next day, Saturday, October 2nd, the people crowded to the meeting ground and organized themselves into their quorums in order. The corner stone of the Nauvoo House was laid that morning; but in the afternoon services in the conference meeting were held.

The Sabbath came—a bleak day; but William and Emeline, with their little ones, were at the meeting grounds, and they saw and heard that day the Prophet of God.

of happiness.

Joseph's sermon was upon the glorious principle of redemption for the dead; and he portrayed the greatness of Divine compassion and benevolence in this plan of human salvation. He said:

"View two brothers—equally intelligent, learned, virtuous and lovely—walking in uprightness and all good conscience, so far as they are able to discern duty from the muddy stream of tradition or from the blotted page of the book of nature. One dies and is buried, never having heard the gospel of reconciliation. To the other the message of salvation is sent; he hears and embraces it and is made the heir of eternal life.

"Shall the one become the partaker of glory and the other be consigned to hopeless perdition? Is there no chance for his escape? Sectarianism answers, 'None, none!' Such an idea is worse than atheism. The truth shall break down and dash in pieces all such bigoted Pharisaism. The sects shall be sifted, the honest-in-heart brought out and the priests left in the midst of their corruption."

Such was the new and exalted nature of the instruction; and when the conference was ended William and Emeline had determined to sacrifice their distant possessions and gather with the Saints in the beautiful city. But their desire was not immediately fulfilled; for William was called to preach and discuss through the States; and in his absence Emeline nobly and cheerfully toiled for her children and their dear father.

Nearly three years of missionary labor, broken by intervals of farm toil, had passed when, on the darkest day of the darkest June ever seen by the summers of this great land, a treasonable massacre took place at the little stone jail in Carthage. The appalling news of this great national crime reached out with sudden horror to all the abiding places of the scattered Saints.

William heard the dread story and hastened home. His

property was fairly given away, and soon he was with his encompassed and persecuted brethren in Nauvoo.

Immediately he was enrolled in the Legion; later he was appointed sergeant; and still later, captain.

I have here the original certificate of his rank as sergeant. The paper is old and the ink is faded; but every letter is legible. It reads:

"May 12th, 1845.

"Greeting:

"This is to certify that William Anderson is appointed first sergeant in the second company, fifth regiment, second cohort of the Nauvoo Legion. And he is therefore to obey all orders and commands of his superior officers with fidelity according to law and military rule and discipline.

"Given under my hand May 12th, 1845.

"Isaac Allred, Capt."

William Anderson and Emeline were faithful; and they received the blessings of the temple. And on "Tuesday of the first week in February, 1846, I [William Anderson] received in marriage in God's Holy House, Drusilla Sargent."

In all the tragic history of the ensuing two years, William was a staunch actor. It was a piteous time! History shows no greater brutality than that which was perpetrated against the city and the Saints, by officially protected mobs; and in the trying days every man was compelled to show his mettle. William Anderson's journal is filled with the record of this awful period. Its simple, unaffected words show how closely allied were the people of Nauvoo to the sublime martyrs of other centuries.

The history of that brief time should be read by every youth in Utah.

On the 10th day of September, 1846—after the cruelly-enforced migration of many of the people of Nauvoo—there were left to guard the city and its remaining population of women and babes, sick and tottering old men—only 123 citizens who were capable to bear arms.

And this was the hour selected by the fiends incarnate for their descent upon Nauvoo. The city was surrounded by an efficiently-armed mob, nearly 2,000 strong; and a bombardment was begun by the besiegers.

When the thunder of the mob's traitorous guns shook the air of Nauvoo, William sprang up to answer the call of duty.

Emeline and Drusilla clung to him—a fearful foreboding of personal evil seemed to take sound and volume with every reverberation of the artillery discharges. But he was firm. He pressed his fond and faithful wives—his helpmeets given him of God—to his martial bosom; and then he left them to solace themselves by prayer while he rushed to the encounter.

Then these two good women—sisters, nay dearer to each other than sisters—knelt down, with arms clasped about each others waists and prayed to the All-Merciful to bring their good husband home in safety from the battle.

One day, two days passed. It was the morning of the 12th day of September, 1846. William was bidding farewell to his wives and his children; when Emeline sobbed anew:

"Oh, my beloved! Let not Augustus go to the battle to-day. He is but a child: think, William! he is only fourteen. Each day he has followed you, taking his gun on his shoulder to fight the wicked enemy and to brave a dreadful death. Let him stay with me!"

Even as she spoke, the thunder of the cannonade shook the city; and William sprang away to hasten to his post, while Augustus gave a ringing cry and fled from the house.

The two women and the little girls were left alone—Emeline and her younger sister wife, the loving Drusilla, and Caroline and Martha—white and trembling.

Hours elapsed, during which these good women were praying as they toiled.

The sounds of the battle waging around the city neither distracted them from devotion nor domestic duty.

Gradually there came a lull; and a momentary hope sprang up in their hearts. But even while the precious thought was taking form, a rattle of musketry shook the window panes; and a moment later the deep boom of a siege gun—shaking the houses from chimney to cellar—told that the struggle was renewed in all its fierceness.

upon the floor. As she dropped she cried:

"Drusilla, my friend, this instant has widowed us and has taken from this house its only son. I feel the dread fact here in my heart!"

The younger wife and the two little girls hastened to the side of Emeline, and there they knelt, weeping and moaning. The premonition seemed too real to be disputed.

While the women and children were rocking back and forth in their agony of apprehension, a hurried knock was heard at the door; and, without waiting for a response, a brother soldier of William stalked into the room. He saw the piteous sight; and all his gallant hardihood gave way. Mingling his heavy tears with the rain from gentler eyes, he sobbed:

"My sister, our Savior help you! Brother Anderson is dead! God's will be done!"

The spirit of courage sustained Emeline, and she cried:

"Where is our husband? Alive he was ours—and we will have his clay now life is ended. Call my boy to bring his father's body home. God's will be done!"

While the grief-shaken soldier was replying, another breathless messenger burst in, saying between his gasps of haste and sorrow:

"Your boy is dead! Oh, Sister Anderson, he fell a martyr —brave, manly, beyond his years—he took a soldier's part: he has met a soldier's fate."

Did this last blow send Emeline swooning? No: in such a crisis a noble, religious soul is exalted beyond the reach of earthly mourning.

Calmly she spoke:

"I will go forth and find our dead—my murdered boy and our martyred husband—Drusilla. Do you prepare couches for their home-coming."

But Drusilla was herself a heroine:

"No, my sister," she said, "your duty is at home. Often your life has been threatened by this mob. They will watch our husband's body, and if you appear you too will be sacri-

remain with these fatherless babes of yours—of ours."

Drusilla rushed from the house as she spoke. Emeline would have followed; but one of her husband's comrades had remained to restrain her, and besides, her little daughters clung at her skirts, determined to prevent her going forth.

So Emeline stayed at the stricken house, preparing for that last solemn home-coming of her soldier spouse and son. While she toiled to fit a bed for the dear forms—now stilled through earthly time—she recalled from her memory that the anniversary of her wedding day was but six days past; and in another fortnight she would be 34 years old—already, in her early prime, she was the widow of a martyr and the mother of a murdered patriot.

Drusilla went abroad through the smoky streets of Nauvoo, escorted by one of the heroic defenders, to the east side of the city. There, resting where he had fallen against a wall, was the bleeding body of her husband. Bravely this fair young woman took from her own shoulders a cloak and laid it across the mangled form.

She breathed a prayer, beseeching strength and courage; and then she sought the place where lay Augustus, the slain son. Tenderly, as if he had been her own boy or brother, she spread her apron over his face.

Then she followed the procession which escorted the bodies of these martyrs to their home.

Who shall speak the agony of the ensuing hours! Two bodies, beloved in life, beloved still in death, were resting in that stricken house. While Emeline and Drusilla; and the little daughters, all robbed of their defenders, wept and moaned in a torture such as seldom comes to womankind.

As she sobbed and prayed, Emeline took from the bosom of her husband a tiny, blood-stained packet. It contained a little flower of hair, Drusilla's, her own and Will's; and also those slips of paper—the hand and heart. The morning when Will first went out to battle, she and Drusilla had pressed this packet upon him and bade him wear it in his bosom.

Emeline pressed the moist hair flower into Drusilla's hand; but the heart and hand, crimson-flecked now, she placed next her own heart. They had been the sign of love in youth and rosy life; they should be cherished to remind her of the immortality which death can bring.

This was almost the end. Emeline's brave boy, Will Anderson, who had given her his fidelity in childhood, had bestowed upon his country his fidelity in manhood. To the oppressed of his countrymen he had extended the help of his strong *hand;* in their defense his *heart* had been pierced by a bullet. He and his son, Augustus, were buried at Nauvoo.

A time of anxious toil ensued; for even through the darkest tragedy runs a thread of the commonplace. And in the midst of the anxious commotion and labor Emeline and Drusilla became separated. They never met again in this life; and from that hour Drusilla's history is to this writer unknown.

Emeline Anderson lived to emigrate to Utah and to receive the blessings of this fair land. She accepted through the remainder of this life the name of a worthy man, and she reared a third daughter. She carried with her until the hour of her death the tear-stained, blood-stained *heart and hand;* and when she was no more, these hallowed shreds of paper passed into the possession of her children.

This is a life sketch. Those of the characters who have gone seem now not to have been torn away by the rude hand of death, but to have faded gently into the past, leaving their looks, their love, their loyalty for their descendants.

A TRIP TO CARSON VALLEY.

By O. B. Huntington.

CHAPTER I.

DESCRIPTION OF THE ROUTE—OBJECT OF THE JOURNEY—CONFRONTED BY INDIANS—DISCOVERY OF RUBIES—MORE INDIANS VISIT CAMP—AN INSPIRED SUGGESTION—THE INDIANS BECOME FRIENDLY.

ON the 18th of September, 1854, I started for Carson Valley, by the advice and consent of Brigham Young, and in the employ of Colonel E. J. Steptoe of the U. S. army.

I went south of the Great Salt Lake and across the then unknown deserts where now are many towns, villages and cities, the settlement of which was hastened some years by that trip of exploration.

The city of Genoa, immediately under the shadow of the Sierra Nevada Mountains, consisting of about a dozen or fifteen houses, was the only actual settlement between Grantsville and Hangtown, California, a distance of one thousand miles by the wagon road over the Goose Creek Mountains, which are one hundred miles north of Salt Lake City; and to find a shorter road so as to save this one hundred miles and to avoid the mountains was the object of my journey.

At the time of which I write this, great mountain country of five hundred miles in each direction from Salt Lake City, was an almost unknown wilderness, a country inhabited only by Indians and wild game, excepting the few settlements of this people; and the country was but little explored, except so far as the wants of the people made it necessary.

Colonel Steptoe was sent by the United States government, with two companies of the U. S. army, as a military governor to take the place of Brigham Young. This was a very quiet, secret movement of our nation to establish a new form of republican government over this people; but thanks to that overruling, inspirational power of God that has so often turned the hearts of men, and the good, honest sense of Col. Steptoe, who, when he had spent eight or nine months with this people, declined the dishonorable and unrepublican office of military governor of Utah. He said that no man but Brigham Young could govern this people, "and if he stepped into Governor Young's place, Brigham Young would still govern the people." He therefore decided to leave for California as early in the Spring of 1855 as he could, and in order to find a new route through south of the Lake he sent an exploring party through to Carson and back that Fall, late as it was.

He applied to Brigham Young for suitable persons for so arduous and hazardous an undertaking. I was chosen as one and was furnished an interpreter (my nephew, C. A. Huntington), and an Indian guide, a young man by the name of Natsab, a son of the Indian chief who was ruler in Salt Lake Valley when we first settled the country—these two were designed to return with me. Besides these was Col. John Reese, now living in Salt Lake City, and he was an excellent companion. His home was in Carson Valley, which at that time was a part of Utah Territory, and he had two men with him, one Willis and a man by the name of Davis, who had been to California, made a raise, returned to the States and was now making his way west again with a very fleet race-horse in hope of opening another "stake" by gambling.

My outfit consisted of six animals to ride and pack, a quantity of goods to use as presents in making peace with the savages we might pass on the way, a good compass to guide us on cloudy days in the deserts and a good quantity of provisions and bedding.

When we had got about two or three miles from Salt Lake City we found eleven men, formerly of Col. Steptoe's outfit of teamsters, camp-followers, etc., who, knowing of our search for a short route to California, determined to sail under the "Mormon" flag as far as Carson.

I had no objections, because their numbers would lend us an appearance of strength among the native tribes. They were rather poorly mounted, armed and provisioned, which latter condition occasioned me eventually some annoyance and suffering, compelling the whole company to live on horseflesh during two hundred and fifty miles of the journey; and during one day and night we were without even that.

For some time nothing of importance occurred on our way, except that we had one horse shot accidentally and one of our strangers lost a mule in a night march across a mud desert.

On the 28th of September, as we were passing through a large valley of meadow land with scattering bunches of tall wheat grass and stools of greasewood, an Indian, naked except for a covering about his loins, with gun in hand, stood before us suddenly and stopped our movements After a very short and unedifying oration he fired his gun in the air, and instantly there arose an Indian from behind every bunch of grass and greasewood all around us until there was quite an army in view, and we saw it was necessary to talk in persuasive tones and our orders were enforced with many presents, in giving which the interpreter was very expert. The Indians guided us to some very fine springs of water and small ponds not far distant, where we distributed quantities of tobacco, pipes, paints, calico, etc.

At this place we passed the night; but in the morning the Indians were all gone, which to men acquainted with Indian natures, indicated hostile intentions, and we therefore traveled cautiously to the west side of the valley, where we nooned at a little creek which came down out of a great range of mountains lying to the east of us, running north and south as far as we could see. Here Mr. Davis said was as good a prospect for gold as any place he had seen in California. We dug a little dirt and washed it out and found several rubies, one very large and fine. We therefore called the place Ruby Valley.

We soon moved on south a few miles; but feeling forbodings of evil, stopped about 2, p.m., on a fine, grassy place near a spring and sent Mr. Davis ahead to reconnoitre the country, which was mostly clear and open to the end of the valley, about twelve miles distant. He rode cautiously about five miles when, on looking over his left shoulder, he saw an Indian on foot running towards the road behind and dropping into the grass as Davis looked around. He instantly wheeled his horse and sped for camp. Just as he started back an Indian on horseback started from some willows near by to cut off his retreat, but that racehorse outran the Indian pony, although the latter had the advantage.

When these facts were known in camp every man prepared for the worst. We had chosen an open piece of ground where we could not be surprised in daylight. We were preparing an early supper so as to have it over before any surprise might be undertaken. Just as we were sitting down to eat, seven Indians on horseback rode slowly towards our camp, came past our horses which were grazing near and dismounted near our fires. We saluted them kindly with "how-de-do," and they replied. They were all dressed in coats, pants, overcoats, caps, etc , and rode well shod horses, excepting one short, thick-set Indian, about twenty-three years old, who wore buckskin pants, a hickory shirt, a Panama hat and with his hair cut short and straight around his neck; he was very wide between the eyes, rode a very large mare without a saddle. He came to my mess where I, my nephew and Natsab were just sitting down to eat, and shook hands.

We sat with guns and pistols in our laps. I told all our company to be very careful, as this one could talk English. The interpreter tried to talk with him, but to no effect until he spoke in the Snake language, when he answered some. They were observing our actions, habits, etc., and making their calculations how and when to take our scalps. I felt that under the Panama hat was a dreadful chief for blood and plunder, and that he could talk English; and I was right in my judgment or feelings.

As soon as the interpreter and I were done eating, we walked around the horses after cautioning the men. While driving the animals a little nearer camp he asked me if I had noticed a secret sign, a strange motion, the Indian made as he shook hands with us, and he showed it to me, stating that he believed these Indians were of the tribe and party who had done so many murders on the Humboldt, among the California gold seekers, and that he believed they were banded with whites by secret oaths, signs and pass-words. Immediately after he told this I felt a strange but bright sensation come over my mind and I could see with my heart, or my spirit could see without my eyes. I told him we would leave the horses and go quickly to camp, where he should go up to that Indian (the chief), give him the same sign he had given us, and that we would then be safe among them.

He did this and the effect was astonishing. The Indian shook hands and hugged him heartily.

I gave further instructions to the interpreter what to say about a certain man whom we knew lived on the Humboldt River, where so much murdering had been done, and with whom I went to school in Nauvoo. Every word had its effect as I anticipated, and the chief understood that this man who lived on the Humboldt, and whom very many believed to be the cause of all the murdering done there for money and plunder, was our friend from boyhood; but the opposite might be said to be nearly true, as we held no sympathy in common, although we had been boys together. The chief called that man his "daddy," meaning father.

CHAPTER II.

Indians' Stratagem to get one of our Horses—Proceed on our Way—How Inspiration is Received—An Illustrative Incident.

We will now leave these few Indians and seventeen white men, all in peaceful, friendly chat, and go back to the 15th of September, 1854—three days before we left Salt Lake City.

On the corner of East Temple Street, just two blocks south of the Temple site was a cottonwood log, on which two young men were sitting in earnest conversation. One was about twenty-four years old, a very tall, muscular man, not less than six feet, two inches in height, with black eyes, set wide apart under a heavy forehead and over high cheek bones. The whole countenance indicated a cruel and heartless disposition. The other young man was just twenty years old, medium height, with a well formed body, small, sharp, twinkling blue eyes, regular features and a rather large head.

They had been quarreling; and when they arose from the log it was agreed that the one who *crossed the other's path should die!*

The older man was to start for his lone log house on the Humboldt, about sixty miles from Ruby Valley, in a week or two, by way of Goose Creek Mountains; and the young man was to start just three days from that time for Carson Valley, as Indian interpreter for a U. S. exploring company, traveling west from Salt Lake City. When we told "Bloody Chief," for such was the name of the chief who visited our camp, that we were special friends to the bad young man we thought not of the terrible consequences that might result from that deceitful stratagem to save our lives then. We told the Indians frankly that we were coming back in a little more than one moon, but did not tell them there would be but three of us.

were merry and jolly, and traded everything they could, and ran foot-races. They wanted to run horses, but ours had too long a journey before them to admit of racing. The main object and effort of the Indians was to get that race-horse, but they did not succeed. They escorted us about eight miles on our way and told us all they could of the country ahead in the direction we wanted to go. They showed us a great deal of gold and silver coin, jewelry and pocket-knives, which they doubtless obtained by killing people on the Humboldt.

We left the valley at the south end, passing over a low divide and through a narrow, rocky canyon, full of scattering cedar trees, making as nice a place for ambush as an Indian could ask for the massacre of whites.

Many incidents occurred worthy of note in a mere narrative; but as I design to show the inspiration of the Lord in our preservation, I shall only give so much of our journey as is necessary to bring you to the circumstances in an easy and natural way. All of God's works are done in a natural way; and He applies a law in one instance which would not do in another. The inspiration of God to different men and to the same man in different ways is a matter upon which I desire to enlarge some little. Sometimes an idea is received in the mind that is foreign to anything that ever existed there before. The person follows that idea, which is so new and to him unusual, and develops a wonderful piece of machinery or a principle in philosophy, manufacturing or something otherwise useful to man. That idea came as other ideas, he will say; but I am of the opinion that it is the inspiration of God that brings out of chaos the very useful inventions and discoveries—this is the simplest form of inspiration.

Another man is perhaps laboring, as usual, in the field and is suddenly inclined in his feelings to go to his house. Perhaps he tries to smother the feeling, but finally yields and reaches home just in time to extinguish a fire that would certainly have consumed his house if he had not gone just as he did.

The inspiration of the Holy Ghost which is given to all who obey the gospel by baptism and the laying on of hands of the Elders, was promised by the Lord to every one that earnestly and sincerely repents of his sins and obeys the gospel, and "it shall guide him into all truth."

I will tell you, my young friends, how that Holy Ghost will guide you. If, when you are made clean from sin by baptism, you do not willingly enter again into sin, pray often, keep the Sabbath day holy, always try as earnestly as you can to be a peacemaker, help every institution of Zion, cheerfully obey every call of the Lord through those who have the authority from God to call, and live lives of purity in every way, that Holy Ghost will be in you all the time and influence you in all your thoughts, words and actions, bring to your mind things forgotten when you need them, and suggest to your mind principle and doctrine, when really necessary, that has never been taught you in this life, but which you knew before you came to this world.

I will mention another incident of inspiration in my own experience, different from the one already related concerning the secret sign among the Indians.

In 1867, I had a friend who was going to San Bernardino, California, and was to start on the second day after the following conversation between us:

"Oliver, come and go to California with me."

"I cannot."

"Yes you can; you can go as well as not."

"I have nothing to leave for the support of my family during the Winter;" (I having been sick for five or six months, and unable to earn anything.)

"I'll lend you what money you want," said he.

"Well, I cannot go, and there is no use thinking or talking about it," I finally replied.

That evening I was going home and thinking of my family affairs, but nothing about going with my friend. A voice, sounding as though it was about a foot from my left ear, whispered:

"Go with Hyrum to California."

The voice was as distinct as any I ever heard, and I half

turned to see if anyone was there, but saw no one; and after debating a short time in my mind decided that I must not refuse, and I said mentally, "Well, I will."

The next day I saw Hyrum and told him I would go with him and I wanted fifty dollars to leave with my wife. He handed me the money and I started with him on the following morning.

My health improved all the way there. I worked at carpenter work all Winter and returned in the Spring, a sound, healthy man.

Other advantages and information gained while gone, prove to me that I was inspired or told to go and do the very thing that was necessary for my present salvation. It was a very important mission to me; and how important no mortal but myself knows.

CHAPTER III.

Out of Provisions—Live on Horse Flesh—Arrival at Carson—Start back for Home—Description of the Journey—Aided by Red Men—Meet with more Indians—Our Manner of Dealing with them.

Three days after leaving our newly-made friends, the Indians, we were on a hard desert, where in one place we crossed a field of crystalized mineral of some kind, which had the appearance of ice, and rode our horses safely over it. That night, on the same desert, one of the fattest horses in the company failed and was left just before we had crossed the desert, and it was nearly morning when we camped. At daylight I sent for the horse to eat, as we were then out of provisions.

The uninvited increase of the company had very small rations at starting, and when their food was exhausted I fed them until there was nothing left to eat for any of us, then we killed the horse and lived on its flesh for one week.

Two days after killing the horse we were on another desert and traveled until far into the night, for we could see no end to the desert; and since living on horseflesh for food we crowded the animals to make the best time possible to get where better food could be had, and more water, for we found water scarce and both men and beasts were in a suffering condition. About 2 o'clock in the morning a stop was made to rest the animals, for they had neither food nor water for over twenty-four hours. The saddles were removed and the animals were turned loose in the desert, where neither bush, stick nor grass could be seen. Being loosened, the animals all began feeding on something, though we could see nothing. We set out a guard, as usual. In the morning we found the horses feeding on a weed or grass of a wine co'or, about four inches high, covering in area about eight acres, and nowhere else did we ever see any more of that kind of feed.

We reached Carson on the 15th of October. We could not start back until word could be got to and from San Francisco. It was getting late in the season and we soon began to feel uneasy about the Winter snows we might encounter, but I had thought of this all the way and took such notes of the route as would enable me to recognize the way again even if the mountains should be covered with snow. I kept what sailors would call a "log book," in which was written a regular description of every landscape—certain-shaped mountains here, a grove of cedars there, etc.; and at every turn of the road, consulted the compass, noting the various directions, and had some certain land-marks at each turn, with estimates of distances between points.

While not otherwise engaged in Genoa, as it is now called, I made a map of the road we had traveled, noting every watering-place, desert, mountain, grove of timber, plot of grass, etc., not forgetting to mark my distances as well as the points of compass.

While at Genoa, Natsab, the Indian, left me one night and started home on foot and alone and made his way in safety.

It was a week before I found which way he had gone, and feared much that the Indians there had killed him. I saw him after I arrived home and asked his reason for leaving me without notice. He said he was afraid we would have to stay all Winter; and that if I had known he was going to leave I would stop him and make him stay too, and that was too long to live among the whites; he would have got sick and perhaps died.

At last the word came from San Francisco, and a man also to go with us to Salt Lake, which was very acceptable. Col. Reece resolved to fit up two men besides himself and accompany me one or two hundred miles, just to explore the country; for of the route we were to take nothing was known by white men, and we were all enthusiastic to search the unexplored regions.

On November 2, 1854, I started for home, with five animals for my own outfit of myself and the interpreter. Our through friend and partner for the trip back, Mr. Kinsey, had two horses, thus making seven well-loaded animals for three men to take care of. One large mule carried a keg of water as a reserve for times of distress. We each carried a canteen of water on our saddles as we rode; and several times our riding horses would, when our canteens were only partly full so that the water would sound as the motion of their bodies shook them, turned and hunted for the water and whinnyed coaxingly for a little sup of the water they had carried so long.

Carson River, at which point Mr. Davis overtook us, sinks or empties into a lake of its own, which is about twenty miles across. Around the lake is a very flat and large extent of country, wet and marshy, which affords great quantities of a grass known as "bayónet grass;" this yields tufts or bunches of black, rich seed that the Indians manage to cut and dry and then thresh or pound out the seed for their Winter's bread. We saw many large-sized stacks of the remains of their threshing at their threshing-floors, which were mostly inaccessible to horses, being on small, dry places in the midst of the sodded marshes that yield the grass.

After passing around the south end of the lake we crossed a low divide and entered a new valley some thirty miles from

twenty feet high and covering from a half to a full acre of ground. In passing among these hills and valleys I saw the heads of two Indians who had not yet seen us. I took in the whole situation at a glance: a large alkali desert was before us in which was no water, while that we had in store was small and poor. Those Indians were not there without water being near, and if we could get them we could perhaps induce them to find or show us water. Our horses in the sand made no noise traveling, so we started at our best speed and soon overtook those whom we wanted as guides. They took us to water, though very reluctantly, and indeed not until they understood that they must do so.

We would never have found the water of ourselves; for the spring was in the top of a little elevation that covered perhaps five acres in the center of a valley. The spring was round and perhaps five feet across. It gave a rapid supply of water, but had no visible outlet. The Indians had fenced it with tall greasewood brush stuck in the ground as thick as they could put it, except at an opening about eight inches wide which would permit rabbits to enter, where they were trapped. A pit about two and one-half feet deep was dug in this opening and a strong, wiry sand-grass was fastened on either side of the hole so that the ends would overlap at the center of the hole or pit, making an apparent smooth floor. When a rabbit jumped on it went down into the pit, which had no water in it. The grass readily sprang back to its place and was prepared for another rabbit. This continued until the pit was full, for it was so narrow and deep there was no chance to jump out. Three similar pits, at a distance from the spring, was prepared for antelope.

We camped here, used the greasewood for cooking supper and refreshed our horses. We kept the Indians all night with us so they could not notify others, who would perhaps prove dangerous. It was the intention to take them a day on the journey, but they escaped when we were not watching them. We traveled, after getting a full supply of water, all that day,

and tend the animals. This long journey was necessary in order to find grass and water.

About half or three-quarters of a mile before coming to the water our animals began to crowd ahead—pull on the bit—which surprised us all, as there were no signs of water, such as willows, trees or grass, in sight to attract our attention, nothing but the smooth desert of small, short desert brush, with occasional fields of sage brush. Suddenly our animals stopped at a little, swift-running brook not more than two or three feet wide.

Here we rested, watered and prepared for our journey. Towards evening we moved about two miles to some low sand hills, which generally afford an excellent grass called sand-grass. The next day we spent in trying to get more easterly over the mountains, but failed.

The second day after watering we would gladly have passed through the range of mountains by a canyon; but thinking it impossible, had started on north again nearly a mile, when someone called behind us. On looking around we saw two Indians running towards us. We waited until they came up. They then enquired where we were going, and on being told, said we would all die if we continued in that direction for it was three days' travel to water. They led us to water in the mountains and stayed with us that night and were well pleased with their newly-made friends, but not more so than we were; for they seemed more like kind old friends, and in the parting got their full share of presents.

On that camp ground I set the compass, but to my surprise one end of the needle dropped down and remained thus. Move the needle where I would it did the same. We were on a mountain of iron and probably some magnetic ore was near.

The next day was the 12th of November, 1854, and by favor of one of these good red men we got through the mountains to a fine, large spring creek, and there camped. Now, who can deny the hand of the Lord and His power in sending these natives with softened hearts to call us from certain death and kindly bring us through to these beautiful springs? None of us did; even the Gentiles with us acknowledged His hand in that act of the savage Indian.

The next morning, Col. Reece, with his two men, left us and turned south to explore three or four days in that direction and then turn westward on their course home. During this journey he made the very important discovery of the Reece River and country now so profitable to the State of Nevada.

We continued our course east one day and a half, and then struck the southern extremity of our outward route, which was a very plain trail at that place and was just at the foot of a long slope approaching a high, rocky, rugged mountain, over which we had to pass.

Indians and snow-storms were alike a dread to us to encounter; and the former were now before us when within about half a mile of the mouth of a very narrow, rocky canyon. They had the advantage of us, for they were nearest the rocks that overhung the road and were on the run in a half-bent posture when first seen on the side of the mountain, but they straightened and sprang to the race right manfully when once in sight, until they were safe among the rocks, where they took positions of safety, only exposing their heads.

We approached slowly, all the while consulting as to what was the best policy to pursue. We did not want to go around the mountain to the south, for of the distance we knew nothing, and to fight we were afraid; for numbers and position were against us, there being only four of us and seven we could see of them. Speaking of four of us reminds me that when eighty miles from Genoa, a man by the name of Davis came to us from California, having heard of the exploring party going to Salt Lake. He had a very large herd of sheep *en route* for California, which was obliged to Winter in Utah, and being anxious to join it he was willing to take chances with us.

The most feasible plan now was to make friends of them with presents. This being decided upon we concluded to try it, and if it failed we must try to force a passage. We consoled ourselves with the saying, "a coward cornered is the worst man in the world to fight." By some means, however, we expected, by the help of the Lord, to get through.

After talking and preaching to the natives half an hour or more the interpreter allured them down near us—so near that presents, small articles we had on our persons, were given them by one of us while the other three guarded against any treacherous surprise. They were then told to go with us to the top of the mountain, where we would camp for the night and we would there give them more valuable articles which were on the horse. They finally consented and told us to go on ahead; but feeling safer with their backs to us than ours to them we succeeded in having them take the lead. They were strong, fierce, desperate-looking men, and we did not care to give them any advantage over us, so we kept our eyes on them and our hands on our guns, even after we had camped at a nice spring in a large opening in the top of the mountain.

Our greatest safety against these and other Indians that might be lurking around, was to take their bows and arrows into our possession, which we did very quietly after giving the promised gifts. They looked rather sorry at seeing themselves entirely in our power.

For our future safety I thought it best to teach our neighbors a lesson in gun tactics, for we felt sure their knowledge of guns was limited to hearsay, they were so very wild and unacquainted with white men. My plan was as follows: I went into a narrow ravine well out of sight, cut a couple of leaves out of my memorandum book, doubled them, shot a hole through the center and then cut them in two. One of these I secretly gave to Mr. Kinsey. The interpreter and I then got into high words. The Indians wanted to know what we were talking about. He told them that I thought I could beat him shooting. They manifested much interest in the matter. I took a leaf from my book, folded and cut it exactly like the first and put it in the split of a stick about three feet long, gave this to Mr. Kinsey, all in plain view of the natives, and he put it up about one-third of a mile off, but exchanged papers on the way and substituted the one with a hole in the center.

The interpreter shot with a dragoon revolver and sent an Indian for the mark. He came back on the run and talking as hard as he could. The Indians all joined in the talk but superstitiously avoided touching the paper.

I could not, of course, shoot better than that and therefore did not try; besides, it was getting dark.

The following morning, which was the 17th of November, one of the natives volunteered to go with us, saying that he "lived over that way." He ran on foot by the side of our horses all day and we rode most of the time on the gallop.

That night, about 1 o'clock, the Indian ran away from the guard—one man with gun in hand—and got clear with his life and two blankets that were not his.

In the morning we found his tracks in the trail ahead of us and we were satisfied that evil was designed against us. We were but a day-and-a-half's ride from the south end of Ruby Valley, and two and one-half days' ride from the north end, where most of the Indians were.

That day, at noon, we came to water on a high ridge, from which I could see a canyon pass through the mountains at the north end of Ruby Valley, which lay north by north-east from us, and the south end nearly east, leaving a great angle or elbow for us to make, which was an object to save. From one place only on this high ridge could be seen this low place in the distant mountains; and as soon as my eyes rested on it the idea was given me that we could get through that pass and save a great distance, and what else it might save I did not know, unless it was our hair. I at once informed the men of the gap in the mountains and my idea that it was best to travel that way; they agreed with me. We turned our horses that way and every one of us felt right sure then that in the plan was our safety.

We traveled that afternoon and until perhaps 12 o'clock in the night and camped on a creek at the foot of the gap, probably ten miles from the top, where we made neither light nor noise.

CHAPTER IV.

Premonitions of Danger—Learn of an Attempt to Kill us—An Indian's Advice—Undecided about what Course to take—Appeal to the Lord—Prayer Answered—Reach Home in Safety.

Early in the morning of the 19th we were in motion, fearing that that day might bring the greatest trial of our lives. Right on the divide we met about fifteen old men, women and children, but none that could draw the bow in battle were there. The interpreter, who was well versed in Indian policies and tactics, said:

"There, boys, that tells the story—not a warrior here and these are sent off out of danger."

We came out into the valley about 2 o'clock very still, slow and cautious, but saw no signs of life near. We had to ride hard so that, if possible, we might get across the valley unobserved. We succeeded, and just as the sun was setting we reached a little basin or valley among low hills on our old trail, where there was a fine spring of water. We looked carefully all over the country behind us as we left the valley, but saw no signs of life except many smokes.

Our hearts nearly came to a standstill as we turned the ridge down into the little basin, at the sight of seven Indians on the run for the water. We had to have the right of water even if necessary to fight for it; and we started on the run. The ground was so open that we could see no point of advantage the Indians could gain by getting to water first, so we rode more leisurely and we came together at the spring.

As they appeared in every motion to be friendly, we dismounted, threw off our saddles and packs as though we were at home, never forgetting to keep our eyes open and revolvers

would talk we could be friends and learn something.

When the oldest man had smoked, he asked in astonishment how we got there.

The interpreter said: "We rode here on our horses."

"Yes," said the old man, "I saw you do that; but what road did you come?"

He was told, and replied:

"That is the only way you could come."

"Why?"

Then he went on to tell us that the Indian, Natsab, who ran away in Carson, had passed there telling when he thought we would be along. The Bloody Chief we saw in the valley going out came all through the valley, calling the men to the rocky canyon that leads out of the valley and there they thought to kill us all and divide the spoils, expecting the whole seventeen men to return.

"Why didn't you go?" was asked.

The old man fumbled among his rags and pulled out a piece of tobacco about one and one-half inches square and said, "I showed him that tobacco and told him you gave me it, and I could not fight you as long as that lasted."

"What if that had all been gone?" was asked.

The old man had as mild and pleasant eyes as I ever saw in an Indian's head, and he raised them with as much honesty and simplicity as a child, after looking in the fire a minute, and said:

"I don't know what I would have done."

His heart seemed to correspond with his eye.

The six men with him were his sons and sons-in-law. He kept them from going to fight us. His camp was about a mile from the spring. After talking awhile we tried the "long shot" game on them and found the paper shot through the center as before. We wanted to impress all Indians with the belief that when they fought us, the farther off they could get the safer they would be.

Then we smoked again and all had lunch. The Indians got

"I do not know whether they will get track of you before morning or not; but they *will* get on your track," said the mild-eyed man. "You must not let the sun see you here. To-morrow when the sun looks down from behind the top of that mountain you must be a long way from here. Ride hard all day; and when night comes, don't stop riding, but ride hard all night, and in the morning you will be in the Goshute land and they will not follow you there. They have long been wanting your meat, and when they find only your tracks they will ride like the wind."

When he had done talking, they all arose with a mild dignity, wrapped their remnants of blankets around them, turned their faces towards their home among the cedars and none looked around, except the mild-eyed man, who gave us a look of mingled pity and hope, then nodded his head towards their home, gave a motion of the hand and a prolonged sigh, as much as to say, "I'm going home to sleep."

The old man's advice to us was carefully followed. I examined my journal and notes of the country before we started. The whole day's travel was over a level country from one valley to another, with no high divide or hardly a separating hill; but at noon I found myself lost, in spite of all my care and even extra caution preparatory for such an important day. I could not find any lack of attention in myself and no responsibility was upon any other person in the matter—the route was very plain, and yet I had gone to the left of a mountain instead of to the right. I knew where we were, although there was no trail on either route, yet I knew we had taken the wrong side of the mountain. I was afraid of the result and questioned whether it would give our pursuers any advantage. Should we turn back or go ahead? was another question.

Our lives was the game we were playing for that day, and the responsibility of correct moves was upon me. The thought made me sweat like rain. I told all the men and asked them to ride slowly, very slowly, while I rode up the mountain to see if I could make any discovery. I rode to a good, secure place and there knelt upon the ground and, with my whole soul, asked God to show me what to do in this trying time of uncertainty.

I arose and mounted my horse, fully satisfied. I knew how it would terminate. An impression, a feeling, some would call it, made me understand this: "Go on; you will come out all right;" that is, keep going as you are going, and you will come around to the right place, was what it meant.

Some might ask, How did you get that information? I can only tell you that it was spoken in those words to my soul. It was planted instantly in my understanding by the power of God. It was revealed to my spirit independent of the body.

I rode down and overtook my fellow-travelers in perfect cheer and told them that we would go on, we were going just right.

Just before sunset we came to the very water I had intended, in the morning, to reach, which was in a nice, grassy vale close by a large cedar grove, and on looking back on the route I designed to come, we saw, on a point of the mountain, three smokes near to each other, which among Indians means to rally to some appointed place. We all, Gentiles though two of the company were, acknowledged the hand of God in guiding us, as we thought, the wrong way.

Water, grass and rest our animals must have in order to carry us safely through the night. We could see the Indian smokes; they could see ours and very likely see us. We must make them think we were going to stay all night, so we drove the horses away from camp quite a distance and towards the Indians, gathered a good lot of wood, ate supper and waited impatiently for the mantle of night to be thrown over our movements.

As soon as I felt sure the Indians' keen eyes could not see our moves through the darkness, two men ran for the horses and drove them around so the fire would not show their forms. The other two men carried the saddles far back from the fire, where we hastily saddled and left the horses in care of one man while the other three went to the fire, put on all the wood and lazily passed and re-passed between the distant

Indians and the fire, then mounted and rode with good speed from our comfortable fire and beautiful Antelope Spring. This place received its name, Antelope Spring, as follows: On approaching this place, as we went west, we saw a drove of antelope feeding just in the edge of the scattering cedars, and one antelope quite a little behind the rest, which one of our men prepared to shoot; but all the animals seeing us ran away. The one behind was thrown into a dreadful fright, and could not run with the others while the man prepared to shoot. He resolved to be an antelope no longer, and with magical power threw off his antelope skin, and in the twinkling of an eye, stood up a tall Indian with bow and arrows in hand. He followed us to camp and there showed us all about the transformation.

We rode all night as fast as we could and at dawn came into a little gulch, where water was found. Here we turned our animals loose and all but two of us laid down and slept until sunrise. That morning was beautiful to us. We now felt ourselves out of danger and quietly pursued our journey homeward, without any other important event occurring. We reached home on the 25th of November, 1854.

This was an important event to us and our families and friends. One thing that made it more important to my wife and relatives was a report from a man who undertook to overtake us a day or two after we left Salt Lake City for Carson. He was a relic of the army, and failing to overtake us as soon as he expected, became faint-hearted from the forbidding and uninviting surroundings of a lone man among Indians and deserts, and turned back. He arrived safely in Salt Lake City and undoubtedly thought himself very fortunate in so doing; and to excuse himself beyond the possibility of reproach among his associates, he made up an inexcusable falsehood and told that he came to the place where the Indians had massacred every one of our party. The deed had just been done and the bodies lay mangled and stripped of clothing. He was obliged to make a hasty retreat to avoid being discovered and served the same.

On arriving in Salt Lake I delivered all U. S. property in my possession to Colonel Steptoe and as soon as possible made my official report in writing and got my release. In my report was given an outline of the road, which, however, he did not think practicable for his army in the following Spring. From my journal of the trip and the map, I formed what was called in those days a guide book, which was a minute account of the road, by which a stranger to the country could safely travel it without danger of being lost.

Our Delegate to Congress then was acquainted with this book, and as he was about to start for Washington by way of San Francisco, he offered to take the guide book and if he could sell it to Congress he would give me half the proceeds. In San Francisco he was offered $1000 for it, but would not let it go for that amount. I think he did not sell it, for I never received any money for it.

GO TO THE

JUVENILE INSTRUCTOR OFFICE,

Salt Lake City, Utah,

FOR

Note and Blank Books, Pencils, Pens, Holders, Inks, Erasers, Rulers, Papeteries, Tabs, Mems., and All Kinds of Stationery.

A Full Line of Publications of Art, Religion, Science, Fiction, etc., etc., for Supplying Public and Private Libraries Always on Hand.

Any Article not in Stock will be Procured on Application.

Book and Job Printing and Binding Done in Excellent Style and at the Lowest Rates.

Subscribe for the

Juvenile Instructor,

An Illustrated, Semi-Monthly Magazine, Only $2.00 per Year, Postpaid.

A. H. CANNON,

(SUCCESSOR TO CANNON & SONS,)

OGDEN CITY, - - - UTAH,

DEALER IN

BOOKS, STATIONERY, TOYS, ETC.

Day School Supplies,
Consisting of Text Books, Slates, Pencils, Note, Blank and Roll Books, Inks, Mucilage, Tabs, Mems., Blackboards and Erasers, Chalk, Maps, Globes, Paper, Book-Keeping Blanks, etc.

All Kinds of Goods for Office use Supplied at the Lowest Rates—Clips, Letter Files, Document Boxes, Invoice Books, Sealing Wax, etc.

Subscriptions Taken for Home and Foreign Newspapers and Magazines.

Libraries of all Kinds can be Supplied with the Choicest Literature at Reasonable Rates.

A Full Stock of Fancy Goods, Sheet Music, Pocket Cutlery, Papeteries, Toys, Diaries, Valentines, Fireworks, Photograph and Autograph Albums, Picture Frames, S. S. Supplies, etc., Always on Hand.

Orders by Mail Solicited, and they will Receive Prompt and Careful Attention.

Dealers can Obtain Goods at the Lowest Wholesale Rates.

BRANCH HOUSE OF THE

Juvenile Instructor Office.

www.ingramcontent.com/pod-product-compliance
Lightning Source LLC
Chambersburg PA
CBHW020859160426
43192CB00007B/985